A BEAUTIFUL MESS

VALERI NOONAN

FOREWORD BY DENNY DURON

ISBN: 978-1-5323-9100-2 (Paperback Edition)
ISBN: 978-1-5323-9101-9 (Hardback Edition)
ISBN: 978-1-5323-9824-7 (eBook Edition)

Library of Congress Control Number: 2018913400

Scriptures taken from the Holy Bible, New International Version®, NIV®. Copyright © 1973, 1978, 1984, 2011 by Biblica, Inc.™ Used by permission of Zondervan. All rights reserved worldwide. www.zondervan.com The "NIV" and "New International Version" are trademarks registered in the United States Patent and Trademark Office by Biblica, Inc.™

Scripture quotations marked (AMP) are taken from the Amplified Bible, Copyright © 1954, 1958, 1962, 1964, 1965, 1987 by The Lockman Foundation. Used by permission.

Scripture taken from the New King James Version®. Copyright © 1982 by Thomas Nelson. Used by permission. All rights reserved.

Scripture quotations marked (NLT) are taken from the Holy Bible, New Living Translation, copyright ©1996, 2004, 2015 by Tyndale House Foundation. Used by permission of Tyndale House Publishers, Inc., Carol Stream, Illinois 60188. All rights reserved.

Editor: Karli Wessale
Editor: Clark Kenyon
Copy Editor: Jeremy Butrous

Book cover art design illustrator copyright © 2018 Chaz Noonan
Book design copyright © 2018 Daniel Del Real

Printed and bound in the United States of America
First printing December 2018

Published by Limitless Ink Publishing
110 Lorton Ave
Burlingame, California

United States of America

To contact the author about speaking at your event please visit www.valerinoonan.com

CONTENTS

DEDICATION

THIS BOOK IS DEDICATED to my husband and best friend in life, Kevin. You are the true definition of the "Proverbs 32 Man," without you, I would never have written this book. I'll never forget the night you told me who the real Proverbs 31 woman was. I have never been the same since. You have been my strength to keep going when I've wanted to quit. You've been my constant encourager, continually helping me believe I could write this book. Thank you for the countless meals, coffee, chocolate deliveries, prayers, and pep talks that kept me writing. I love and adore you with every fiber of my being, I am so excited we get to share this incredible message to the world together. This is our first book, baby!

To my amazing children, Kelci, Kassidi, and Chaz. Thank you for being my greatest inspirations in life. I love you with my entire heart and soul. I admire and adore each one of you. You three are constant reminders of God's love. I am so thankful He chose me to be your mom. As C. S. Lewis said, "Children grow much faster than books." I can't believe when I started this project, you kids were only sixteen, ten, and seven. Now at the completion of this project, eight years later, you are twenty-four, eighteen, and fifteen. Thank you for all your support and encouragement during the process. Each one of you played a crucial role in helping me get to the finish line. We finally made it! Now it's time to celebrate!

To my precious mama, who went to be with Jesus during this project. You were always my biggest cheerleader in life. I know you've been with me through this entire process. Before you left for heaven, I promised you I would finish this book. The day I completed it was exactly a year to the day that you graduated to heaven. I love you mommy, this book is for you!

To my dad, who has been in heaven for twenty-eight years now, yet is more alive than ever in my heart and life. Thank you for all you taught me about faith, and prayer. As they say, "More is caught than taught." You are my hero of the faith, I love you.

FOREWORD

I first met Valeri Noonan when she was a teenager and I was speaking at the great Hilltop Community Church in Richmond, California, where her dad was the lead pastor.

From the time she was a young girl, Valeri has had a heart for God. In the years since, I have come to know her as an exemplary wife, mom, and Christian minister.

But after all this time, I have most recently become acquainted with Valeri Noonan the Author. I am extremely impressed, to say the least. She has written a book that I feel will become well known throughout the Christian world, especially in the ever-expanding circles of women's conferences and ministries. This is a good read and would be the perfect "First book of the year" study for you and your small group.

A Beautiful Mess is beautifully written and the message is beautifully redemptive. Who would dare to take on the Proverbs 31 woman? Valeri's research, analysis, and gut-honest candor undoubtedly give the reader the clearest, most attainable view of this iconic woman yet. I recommend this book almost as highly as I recommend you get to know its author. I sure hope there are more Valeri Noonan books to come.

Denny Duron

CHAPTER ONE

Hidden in Plain Sight

IF ANYONE TOLD ME I would be writing a book about the "Proverbs 31 Woman," I would have laughed in their face. This woman is the last woman in the Bible I would choose to write about. However, growing up in church, I was taught she is the ultimate woman - greatly praised and honored by God. Myself, along with many other women, have been taught she is the woman we should all strive to be like.

She is the perfect woman of God. Yet, anytime I read about her, or heard teachings about her, it completely stressed me out. She is ridiculous! Come on ladies, if we are honest with each other we wouldn't even choose to be her friend. She isn't human, she can't be. This is the woman the Bible says, "Never brings her husband harm, only good, all the days of her life." It also tells how she sews (with eager, beautifully manicured hands) into the wee hours of the night, while the rest of the family is sleeping. She's sewing clothes for her family, her servants, and herself. She also sews her bedding and the bedding of those in her family. Once she finishes sewing for half the night, she's up before the sun to prepare breakfast for her family. No doubt she is dressed, hair done, makeup on as she serves her well-rested family breakfast with a smile. She is also a shrewd business woman who purchases land at such a great steal she has money left over to plant a vineyard on it. She is also the woman who is never striving and never stressed out. She is able to laugh at the days to come. She is clothed in strength and dignity, and her children rise and call her blessed. Her husband also blesses and honors her.

Who is this lady? There is no measuring up to this super woman. Honestly, who wants to be this woman? I know I have never wanted to be her. I like to sleep in and have fun. I like to take an easy day (or two, or three). I like to order take out. I love it when my husband tells me he will take care of dinner for the night. Isn't it good parenting to train my darling children to make a meal and clean it up? I don't want to be the last one to bed every night, and the first one up every morning. There's no way I am going to be able to make my own bedding, clothes, and my family's clothes. I don't want to make any clothes, ever! This woman can't be a real woman. She is a Stepford Wife. There isn't any part of her I can relate with. I think that is what makes it so difficult. I don't relate with her at all.

The biggest struggle of all, for me, was the fact that I thought God expected me to be like her, or even worse, expected me to be her. If that was true, I was already disqualified. There is no way I could ever come close to this woman. But maybe if I continued to pray, read my Bible, and work harder, perhaps I could somehow figure it out. I truly thought this was what God considered a woman of worth. The ultimate wife, ultimate mother, ultimate career woman – the super-woman of the Bible, God's woman. She is conveyed as the only woman in the Bible to figure it all out, and do it perfectly. Her play book is there for all women to follow.

Men, maybe if there was a Proverbs 32 Man that you had to live up to, it would be easier to understand my angst with this woman. What if the Proverbs 32 Man was just as unachievable? The man with the perfectly chiseled muscles, and six-pack abs. He has a seven-figure salary and he is the perfect romancer. He never misunderstands his wife when she is needing him to hear her heart. He is always home for dinner by five. After dinner he tells his wife to go kick her feet up and read her favorite book while he and the kids do the dishes. He eagerly steps in to make sure the kids complete their homework, take their baths, and are tucked into bed right on time. He is able to drop the kids off at school on his way to work in the morning. He never gets distracted when his wife needs his full attention. He does laundry, he cooks, he cleans, and he knows what his wife wants even before she asks. He is the best at everything he sets his mind to. Even his profits earn profits. He is kind, successful, handsome, and respected by all. His children rise and call him blessed. It isn't achievable. Imagine feeling like God expected that of you? That is how so many women have viewed Proverbs 31. How does one ever measure up?

Who is the one describing her? Who is the author of this portion of scripture? Did he really know her? Does anyone know who this woman is? The answer to these questions is what compelled me to write this book. The answer to these questions has changed my church going, pastor's daughter, pastor's wife, Christian since I was born life. I am forever changed because of the true identity of this woman. I have gone from hating her, to greatly admiring her. She is my role model. She is my inspiration of how to be a true woman of dignity and virtue. She has shown me that no matter what I face, I can make it through, and make it through strong.

You are going to get to know a woman who has been misunderstood, overlooked, rejected, shamed, scorned, wrongly accused, and devastated by pain. She has known abuse, loss, fear, hopelessness, and grief beyond words. She has been dishonored and stripped of everything she once held dear. Yet somehow, this woman stood tall, and never gave up. She was clothed in dignity, and she was able to laugh at the days to come. She went from complete loss, to being given the place of highest honor a woman could hold. I can't wait for you to meet her, and for her to finally be known for who she really is. "A woman who surpasses them all. She deserves the reward she has earned, let her works bring her praise at the city gate. This woman who fears the Lord is to be greatly praised!" (Proverbs 31:29-31 NIV). She has forever changed the way I see God and how He loves me. You don't have to be Christian to read this book. This book is for everyone. I promise you won't be disappointed but you will be surprised! Mostly, I hope and pray this will encourage, empower, and challenge you the way it has me.

It was a Thursday night, the night Kevin and I set aside during a very busy season of life we were in. Thursday night was the finish line we could look forward to at the end of the week. It wasn't usually anything very fancy. It was just one night of the week we could count on to be together, just the two of us. This particular Thursday night we were eating at one of our favorite spots in Berkeley, an Indian restaurant called The Mint Leaf. We loved the ambiance of the live jazz band playing in the background of the cozy dimly lit restaurant. During that time in our lives, my husband Kevin and I made it a point to keep weekly date nights, because if we were not intentional about taking time to spend together, it wouldn't happen. At the time, we had a 7-year-old son, a 10-year-old daughter, and a 15-year-old daughter. Raising children and keeping a house is a challenge in and of itself, but we were also pastoring a brand new church campus. If that wasn't enough to juggle already (which, let me tell you, it felt like enough), I was back in school full-time. I had a dream to become a counselor because I wanted to be professionally, as well as spiritually, equipped to help people in the most challenging times in their lives. I knew I was called to bring hope to people that were locked in prisons of bondage and shame and to help equip them to walk out of those prisons. But as we all know, there is no good time to go back to school full-time when you are older and have many other responsibilities that you can't put on hold. However, I knew God had put His finger on my heart; and I knew it was time. When I say God put His finger on my heart, it is just what He did.

It happened when I was at a women and children's home called Teen Challenge. My husband and I were there to tour the house. Our church was preparing to do a home makeover for the girls and we were getting our task list ready. This was a home where girls could come who had lost all hope. They could bring their kids along, as well, if they had children. Or if they were pregnant they would receive the help they needed to have the baby safely. They were usually drug and alcohol addicted. They were victims of abuse. They needed a lot of help. The children were able to live there while their mothers detoxed and completed the program. I loved going over to that house and loving on those girls. The funny thing was, every time I was there, I felt more like they were ministering to me, rather than me to them. Watching the transformation from week to week was amazing. You could see such a difference in the countenance of the new girls from the ones who had been there awhile. At first they came in addicted and closed off emotionally. Most of them were non-responsive and cold. Then you would see the softening begin. Just to look at the face of a girl from week to week and see the change happening was incredible. I always tell people, if you ever want to find the heart of God, go visit a place like that. You are guaranteed to feel the heart of Jesus in that place.

As we were walking, I made the comment that I wanted so desperately for these girls to have access to professional counseling. It was funny because it was just after I said this, as we were walking through the house taking notes, that something hit me like a truck. I started crying uncontrollably. I was embarrassed because I could not shut it off. I tried to hide it, but my husband saw me. He looked at me and said, "Val, are you okay?" I couldn't really answer. I just nodded my head with a yes. I could usually suck it up and hide my emotions enough to get through, but it became more and more difficult to hide. Our friend noticed as well and asked if I was okay. I just said, "My heart just breaks for these girls." I finally pulled it together. But what no one knew was that I had just felt the power of God touch my heart like I had not felt it before.

I shared with my husband what happened once we got in the car to head home. I told him, "Kevin, I heard God speak to me so loud and clearly with no audible words necessary. It was like God pressed His finger onto my heart and said, "When are you going to do it, Valeri? You say you want to help people that are stuck and without hope. You said you wanted to get your degree so you could have the tools to professionally help these people. So, when are you going to get your education and do it?" I knew I had to go back to school. I knew God had just called me back. And He wasn't saying later, He was saying now! When I say God called me back, I mean back to ground zero. I told Kevin I had to go get registered for college. He looked at me and said, "Now?" I looked right back at him and said, "Now!" I literally went home and started the process. I was scared and had no idea how I was going to do this. I never liked school, hence why I was starting at ground zero in my late thirties. But with Kevin's support and a lot of courage, I went back to the junior college near our home. I had to finish my general education, and then go on to University where I received a Bachelor of Science in Counseling Psychology with a minor in Biblical Theology, and I was able to integrate a two-year certification in addiction studies into my degree as well. Yes, I did it! I have to celebrate that whenever possible. It seemed like I was never going to finish school. It took me five years. But I did it! When God calls you to something, it really doesn't have to make sense. It just has to be done. He is the one that will make sense of it for you. All you are called to do is take the step that is in front of you, until there are no more steps to take.

Needless to say, we were in a very busy time in our lives. So, we valued our date nights very much. This particular night, however, was one that stopped me in my tracks, and changed my life forever. As we sat at our favorite table in the back, right corner of the restaurant, under the cool hanging blue lights, Kevin said something that would change my life forever. He said, "I was thinking about Mother's Day Sunday, and I want to go a different direction with the message." I, of course, replied by asking, "What do you mean?" He replied, "I was thinking it would be cool to talk about the Proverbs 31 woman, the virtuous woman." To that I replied, "What?! Why? Why would you want to do that to women on Mother's Day?" He of course said, "What are you talking about?" I said, "Kevin, let me be honest, I can't stand that lady. I'm sorry, I know she's in the Bible, and we should all be striving to be just like her, but quite frankly, I think she's the last person real women want to hear about on Mother's Day. The perfect woman. The woman is ridiculous! These poor ladies are coming to church on the one day that they get to have the focus on them. They hopefully don't have to (but more than likely will) get the kids ready and out the door to church. Hopefully her family will take her out to a nice lunch and pamper her with some nice gifts and tell her what a great job she is doing as a wife and mommy. However, most won't feel like they're even close to being a good enough wife, mom, or even woman for that matter. Most will leave behind a house that looks like a tornado went through it while they were at church. They will face loads of laundry, dishes, and a Monday routine of barely getting the kids out the door on time, fed, and with matching shoes. Some may have had a fight with their husbands. Some may have just yelled at their kids before entering the parking lot. Yet, we are going to sit up there on the stage and share this perfectly nauseating account of the "Perfect woman" that scripture tells us we should all achieve to be. Most women will then feel even worse about the things they aren't doing, aren't measuring up to, and on top of it all, God is the one that is putting this expectation on them. "No. I'm sorry Kev, I can't do it."

The truth is, I haven't just been bothered with this "Virtuous Woman" in the Bible. I couldn't stand her. There I said it. Yep, I did not like her, I thought she was ridiculous. I also thought that she was the reason many women would be turned off to God. Why do I say such blasphemous things? Why would I ever say such disrespectable ungodly things about a woman the Bible holds in such high esteem? I'm glad you asked! So, let's start by going back to the restaurant.

Kevin gently smiled and let me vent and carry on about all these things I felt, because he already knew I would most likely react when he brought this up, and then when I was finished he asked me a question I will never forget as long as I live. He said, "Val, do you know who she is?" I said, "No one knows who she is, she isn't an actual person." He said, "That is not true. We do know who she is." I said, "What are you talking about?" He then proceeded to tell me why he was wanting to change the original message he was going to preach on Mother's Day and share about her instead. What he said next rocked me to my core. It rocked my Christian, church-going, pastor's daughter, Bible story reading since I was born life. He told me he had been doing some study on Proverbs 31. He began to look deeper into the account of the virtuous woman. He went on to say, "Do you know who King Lemuel is?" I, of course, said, "No, why?"

He said the header (title) of Proverbs 31 reads, "The Sayings of King Lemuel." He went on to tell me that after a lot of research he discovered very plainly the identity of King Lemuel. And with this new discovery it made talking about the virtuous woman much more interesting. So, I of course asked, "Well, who

is he?" He said, "King Lemuel is Solomon." Lemuel
is most likely a name that his mother called him. It
is a Hebrew name for a baby boy. The meaning is,
devoted to God and loved by God. She was basically
saying, my gift from God, my boy loved by God.
It was a term of endearment many scholars say, his
mother's pet name for him. So, I guess it would make
sense that he would use the name his mother called
him when writing this Proverb about her. But wait
a minute. If Solomon is Lemuel, then his mother
must be, Bathsheba? If Bathsheba is the woman he
is referring to when he says, "The sayings of King
Lemuel contain this message, which his mother taught
him." He is talking about Bathsheba? What he said
next changed my life forever, including the way I read
the Bible and the way I see God. Everything changed
with this one sentence. Kevin looked at me and said,
"Val, Bathsheba is the Proverbs 31 woman." I just
stared at him, and then said, "There is no way that
is true." We both grew up in church. I am a pastor's
daughter. I have never one time in all my life heard
anything close to this. She was the adulterous woman.
Not just church going people know who this woman
is. She is known throughout the world as the woman
who had an affair with King David. There are famous
paintings of Bathsheba. One by the famous Dutch
artist, Rembrandt, that hangs in the Louvre in Paris.

He finished the painting in 1654. The header says, "Bathsheba at Her Bath", the title of the painting is, "Bathsheba with David's Letter." Another painting titled "Bathsheba at Bath" dated around 1575 painted by Italian Renaissance painter Paolo Veronese hangs in the Musée des Beaux-Arts de Lyon, France. This is not just any woman. She is known throughout world history as the scandalous woman. The woman that made King David fall. This was a big deal. He smiled and said, "It's true." I started crying. I didn't even try to hide it. I was just crying. I can only tell you that the message of this even possibly being true made something deep inside my soul begin to cry.

"It's Bathsheba." Kevin said. "Proverbs 31 is an epilogue Solomon wrote about Bathsheba, his mom. In epilogues, the writer is allowed to incorporate their personal commentary about a person. Solomon was sharing from his perception, his personal thoughts and feelings about his mother. His mother was his tutor, along with Nathan the prophet. The beginning of Proverbs 31 is the teachings of his mother. The first words of the chapter are the wisdom she taught him. Her words, which God Himself saw fit to include in scripture, will help us all learn. When you read about how the Proverbs 31 woman can do no wrong, that is from Solomon's perspective."

I couldn't stop crying. I didn't believe that

Bathsheba could be the virtuous woman, but I longed so desperately for it to be true! If true, this was a game-changer. I thought about my little boy, Chaz, who was seven at the time. My son thought I was perfect and the most beautiful woman in the world. When he was really little he would tell me he wanted to marry me. He was so protective of me. I loved the version of me I saw when I looked at myself through my son's adoring eyes. I did feel beautiful, adored, like I was the only person on the planet. I was enough.

Kevin reminded me of the card my son had given me with an acrostic for Mother's Day. It described me as if I was the perfect mom. It said things like, "My mom makes me pancakes, eggs, and sausage for breakfast every morning. My mom organizes my toys and always keeps my room and the whole house clean, my mom talks to me every night until my problems are gone, my mom has the prettiest hair in the world." I laughed later when reading the card again because I couldn't help thinking how Chaz sees me as so much better than I knew I was. Although, I did keep reading that card over again, I knew I wasn't the perfect mom he was describing. Still, something in me so enjoyed being "her", even if it was just for the time I read the card and allowed myself to believe it. He didn't know the narrative I was listening to the rest of the time. The one that tells me the version of the mom I "really" am. The one of the mom in the kitchen with crazy hair, trying to gulp down my triple shot espresso in order to open my eyes enough to deliver that beautiful breakfast. The mom pulling frozen pancakes and sausage out of the freezer and throwing them into the microwave and spinning a few eggs around on the stove. Barely getting it done in enough time so my boy could eat before running out the door to school.

Chaz only saw a homemade breakfast just for him, right on time, delivered on his favorite "Lightening McQueen" plate, with orange juice in his favorite "Mater" cup, lovingly placed on his favorite matching placemat. He saw this from the only woman in the world that made breakfast like that, every day, just for him. So when my husband told me that is how Solomon saw his mother, my heart said, "Oh. Yes! I get it! That is what it is!" I knew it could be true because I had experienced it.

So my friends, that is the moment that changed my life forever. I have never been the same; it rocked me to my core. I am not being dramatic or trying to create a buildup or drama. It is a genuine moment that created an upheaval in my spirit, and created a radically different, better understanding of God and the scriptures. I believe the revelations that came from this moment, will do the same for you! That was the moment I felt shame and fear drop off of me and I stopped trying to compare myself to perfection. I was no longer trying to compete with some wonder woman I read about in the Bible. The woman who served as a constant reminder of how I wasn't enough, and I never would be. Worst of all, feeling like this is the woman that God expected me to be. I was no longer judging myself as such a failure. I learned it is okay to have a mess in our lives and still be seen by God as beautiful. I went home and let me tell you, I started digging! Suddenly, I did not want to work on my papers for school and study for exams. Instead, I stayed up late studying Bathsheba; the woman who now made me feel okay about being imperfect and having messes in my life.

She has inspired this book. I feel inadequate to be the person to deliver this message about a woman who is so unbelievably amazing. I grew up hearing how terrible she was. I was taught she caused David to fall and caused him to sin. I formed a picture in my mind of her bathing on her rooftop fully aware David was looking on. She was intentional about seducing him. But, I know now, that she has been lied about through the course of history. She has been misrepresented.

The truth about Bathsheba has been hidden in plain sight. Some might say behind false narratives and bad theology. Or maybe we just haven't taken the time to look a little closer at the truth. I want to invite you to open your eyes in a new way as you go on this journey of discovery with me. In the end, you can decide for yourself.

The Bible does not say anything about her bad character which I had grown up hearing about. It does show us quite a bit about her character, and about who she was. However, not one bit of evidence points to her being anything but virtuous. Most of what is said about her, comes from a prophet named Nathan. God used prophets in the Old Testament to speak to the people on His behalf. We will look directly at the scriptures that tell the story of David and Bathsheba. We will read the rebuke brought to David from God, through the prophet Nathan. God gives us a very clear message of who Bathsheba is, and what really happened in the account of David and Bathsheba. The Bible tells us everything we need to know. The lie about Bathsheba's identity is what most of us have believed to be truth. Just as the lie about our identity could become what we believe is true. How does this happen? How could we believe a lie even about our own identity?

There is an enemy of our soul. He wants nothing

more than to get us to align with the lie he wants to write over our hearts. Is there a narrative you have believed? Is he trying to get you to identify with a false identity? His goal is to put a robe of shame over your true identity so you will miss the real title God has always placed over you. Titles of truth, such as, loved, perfect, beautiful, virtuous, noble, enough. That really is what God says about you and me. That is what He always said about Bathsheba as well. Bathsheba's life reveals a beautiful mess, and her story can teach us about the heart of God. God's heart is to set the captive woman and man free and see us walk in our true identity in Him.

As I take you on this journey of unveiling the true identity of the virtuous woman, Bathsheba, we will get to know King David in a fresh way. Possibly a different side of David than many have ever seen. We will also get to know Solomon, their beloved son, chosen by God to be the next King of Israel. Bathsheba's family. David's family. We will begin to see a common thread that weaves through all of our lives. I will share parts of my beautiful mess with you. I believe you will also find yourself and your messes of life being woven together into this marvelous thing called humanity. The beautiful mess called life. My desire is that as you read about these real people and how God never gave up on them, never stopped loving them, you will see how much God loves you, even in the middle of your mess. If you gain anything from this book, as you read, I hope you become convinced that no mess - not yours, not mine, not the one you were born into, forced into, or walked into - will separate you from the love and delight God has for you! None of that can separate you from your true identity in God, or from fulfilling your God-designed destiny.

~ CHAPTER TWO ~

Separating the Truth from the Trash

EVERY MESS INCLUDES PROMISE, power, and choices. God has our gifts and victory waiting for us in the mess, if we trust and look to Him for redemption. My hope is you will gain a new understanding of how God never leaves you during the desolate times of your life. I hope God shows you how during the bad times, those are the times you are being primed to be elevated up and beyond. He never allows anything to touch us, or to hurt us, if it hasn't already been approved by Him to ultimately bring good to us. It can become the most beautiful gift God gives you. Our mess is not something to completely forget or push secretly aside. It is something to accept and be thankful for. We can learn to compartmentalize our messiness just like we do with material things.

When I need to clean a closet, garage, or even something as small as a drawer, the first thing I need is the right containers to separate the trash from the things I want to keep or give away. That is what makes cleaning a mess so much easier. A place to put everything. Garbage goes in the 'trash' container. Things I want to give away go into the 'give- away' container. Things loaned to me go into the 'return' container. Things I want to keep go into the 'keep it' container. This makes it so easy to sort because now I have somewhere for everything to go. Instead of facing a huge overwhelming pile and not knowing where to begin, I am empowered and motivated because I have a plan. I am intentional about every item. I am the one in control of the mess instead of the mess taking control of me. And when I am finished I know exactly what I do and do not have. There are no surprises and I don't have to worry that someone might see my mess. I am the one managing my stuff. I know where to go if I need something. And I know right where to put things when I want to clean up quickly. It feels so good to be organized. Nothing is better than knowing right where everything is. I feel happier and lighter. I also feel more at ease when people are around. Because I'm not worried about hiding my mess, I have peace. There is so much peace that comes from not hiding your mess, or being buried under your mess.

I have always told my kids, if everything you own has a home, you won't have stragglers in your room. In other words, every toy needs to go home when you're done with it, or else your room will become so messy you won't be able to enjoy anything. It is the same principle with our emotional, spiritual, and mental stuff. We need to pull it all out and look at it. Then we need to determine what is garbage, and what is of value, and what we need to give away. A very important container that many leave out is the 'return' container. In my years as a counselor I have found this to be the biggest container we should buy. When I began my counseling practice, I quickly discovered there is a root issue that almost all other issues stem from. It is also the most difficult problem to detect because it has been falsely identified as love. It is deadly. It is powerful, and it destroys lives.

This problem is actually a disease. It is more powerful than any substance. It is called codependency. This is when we live with the motto, "I'm okay, you're okay, I'm not okay, you're not okay." Simply put, the codependent person bases their own feelings of happiness and self-worth upon the acceptance and approval of others. The problem with codependency is it renders us completely powerless. We are not responsible for how anyone else thinks, feels, or behaves. We are only responsible for how we think, feel, and behave. Unfortunately, countless people will never live life to the full, the way God intended, because they will never adopt and apply this simple truth. Any person I have counseled or coached that has applied this truth to their life has experienced incredible breakthrough, even in those seemingly impossible relationships in their lives. You know the relationships with people where no matter what you try, it is never enough. The people with whom you feel like you're always walking on egg shells. The people who somehow have the power to make you feel it is your responsibility to make them happy.

It is incredible to watch the healing that takes place when an individual takes their power back and applies this truth to their life. It is like watching big stone walls come down from around them and they walk away free. Sadly, many don't choose to do the work to get free, and they go on to live in partial freedom. I've seen both. I am happy to tell you, I did the hard work and it works. Life to the full really does exist. It won't keep your life mess-free forever, just as those containers won't keep you from accumulating clutter again.

It is the continual process of being intentional about putting things where they belong. It requires periodically dumping our containers out and re-organizing because we allowed some things in that didn't belong. Returning guilt, shame, expectations, and abuse are a few of the big ones. Those don't belong to you. If someone has loaned you their opinion of you, their expectation of you, or their power over you, it is your responsibility to put those in the 'return' container. It is important to remember this is your responsibility. You have the power to give it back.

No one has the power to make you mad. We choose to become angry with what someone says, or does. We can just as easily choose to not become angry. We waste time trying to figure out what someone else is thinking, when we can choose to allow the other person to think whatever they want, it is their choice. What they think doesn't change anything, if we don't allow it. We can choose to give it back. You can choose to not allow someone else's bad attitude or how they think you should act, think, or feel, affect you. You can simply get the 'return' container out and place it there. An example of that would be, "I'm sorry you feel that way, but that is not truth." You can respect a person, even a person you don't like, without allowing them to take your power. God gives us the power to apply this, "For God did not give us a spirit of timidity *or* cowardice *or* fear, but [He has given us a spirit] of power and of love and of sound judgment *and* personal discipline [abilities that result in a calm, well-balanced mind and self-control]" (2 Timothy1:7 AMP).

These feelings of guilt, pressure, shame, and how you "ought" to do things, are stragglers. They are clutter. They will keep you in a mess, and eventually make you a mess. God doesn't make us feel guilty, shamed, or condemned - no one has the power to make you feel guilty, shamed, or condemned unless you give them the power. The only person that has the right to make you feel guilty is the Holy Spirit. However, it is not a guilt that causes feelings of shame or condemnation. It is conviction, not guilt, that compels us back to the heart of God, because we are sorry and want to make it right. I like to put it this way: anytime I feel fear, shame, confusion, condemnation, insecure, or bad about myself, I know it isn't coming from God. His desire is for us to feel secure in His love, regardless of what we have done. When we begin to accept the unconditional love that God offers us through Jesus, it will compel us to want to change our behavior. We will feel bad because we know what we are doing hurts the heart of God. The reason it hurts God is because He knows how badly it hurts us. The enemy wants you to think God doesn't love you anymore, or that you've been rejected by God because of something you've done, or maybe something you haven't done. Learn to recognize the truth from the lies. God is not like people, He never changes. He is a good father. You can't do anything that will separate you from His love. That is truth.

As we look more closely at the lives of Bathsheba and David we will see just how important it is to apply this truth to our circumstances. Here we will see two people caught in the same terrible situation. One is guilty, the other is not. Both have choices to make. One has to learn to walk in believing they are forgiven, and the other has to continue to walk in forgiveness towards the other. We will find ourselves in both of these people - David and Bathsheba. Two individuals who have to remember what God says about their true identity, not listening to what others think or say about them. And they must keep their own minds from going back to old narratives and instead, staying aligned with the truth of what God thinks and says about them.

We can't function with stragglers in our heart and mind or else the clutter will keep us from being able to enjoy life. I like to ask myself if what I am believing about something is actual truth, or just a belief system I have been programmed to think is true. An unhealthy belief system can be the road block that keeps you from living life to the full. We need to make sure we keep truth as our guide as we check the inventory of our "B.S." belief systems. Do you have some "B.S." you might need to throw into the garbage? Or return to sender? Our beliefs are not always truth. They are just that, a belief. A thought is just a thought until you come into agreement with it. Once you agree with the thought it becomes a belief. Once you believe something long enough, it becomes truth to you. Some false belief may have made its way into your truth container.

I hope this book will help you in separating the truth from the "B.S." in your life and into the containers it belongs in. Once you begin to think for yourself, and allow the ultimate truth of Jesus in to help you, you will be able to organize the drawers, closets, and even the garages of your heart. Once things are cleaned out and compartmentalized you will see there is more room in there than you thought. Now there is open space. The space that Jesus wants to fill up with his love, peace, and purpose for your life. We can get the messiness of our life cleaned up and organized into the appropriate containers. We label the container with truth, we then put it on the shelf of victory. When needed, we can pull it down and share it with someone who needs the hope our mess can bring to theirs. The only person capable of controlling outcomes is God; however, He will never manipulate the outcome. He gives us the ability to choose. So why do we think we are more powerful than God, and that we somehow control whether or not a person is happy or sad? Or, that what we do or say has the power to control the outcome of another person's life. Why do we give our power to others, by letting them control the outcome in our lives? No one has the power to make you happy, sad, mad, or even a victim. You choose whether you come into agreement with those things. You can choose every day to keep your power. When you base your happiness, your joy, your security, or your identity on what other people think, feel, or say about you, you have just given your power away to them. You won't be able to live the fulfilled life God designed for you to live until the only person you check in with is Him.

God never asks you to hide anything. People do. If God still loves you, and God can handle your mess, who cares if someone else can't. It is their responsibility to take that up with God. God left all the dirty details in the Bible for a reason. He is a master at making dirty, messy things into invaluable beauty.

Since the evening my husband told me about the Proverbs 31 woman, God deposited a passion in my heart to share it with everyone I can. It set me on an exciting road of researching everything I could get my hands on that pertained to this woman and her family. It re-energized my tired soul. I have discovered things that have absolutely blown my mind. I am so glad to share this amazing discovery with you. In no way am I asking you to take what I say as gospel. I just want to take you on the journey I've been on so you might experience a similar revelation.

As you take this journey with me, my desire is for you to become inspired, challenged, and excited to rise to new levels in your life. New levels in your relationship with God, others, and yourself. You will find the powerful freedom of being fully known and loved. Accepting the truth that if God can handle the whole you, it doesn't matter what anyone else thinks. You will throw off the false labels and titles of shame the enemy has written over your heart. You will discover your true identity in Christ - seeing yourself the way God truly sees you. You will begin to accept and receive everything that is rightfully yours. Understanding when you have Jesus, you hold the same power within you that was used to raise Him from the dead. Therefore, you have been given all the power you need to live this beautiful mess called life, to the full.

I am so excited to begin this journey with you. It is a journey through this *Beautiful Mess* called life. I will share some of my beautiful mess, along with the beautiful mess from the story of Bathsheba and David. Hopefully, you will find the truth that is hidden in plain sight. I hope you discover that we all have a beautiful mess to share. We need each other. We need to be safe to share the mess along with the beauty. When you have one without the other, it just doesn't work. No one wants to be around someone who is just a mess any more than someone who is "perfect." The beauty is seeing someone who has faced difficulties, failures, and hardship and somehow, they've come through it better and stronger than before. I know people who radiate beauty from their very being. Some of these people have gone through unmentionable pain, suffering, and devastation in their lives. However, because they allowed the mess to make them better, they stand even higher than many people who haven't gone through such difficulties. They are full of joy, kindness, and understanding for others. Each time we come through a difficult season stronger, we have essentially put that mess under our feet. The mess then serves to elevate the beauty. We stand taller because of what we stand upon. The platform of victory. I don't know of a powerful influencer for Jesus whose platform wasn't built out of a mess that was transformed into beauty by Jesus. The more mess we conquer and put under our feet, the more beauty will be elevated. If we don't have any messiness to share with others we really don't have much to offer. You see, our pain is what connects our hearts to one another. Our victory over the pain is what causes others to believe there is hope for what they are going through. It brings life back into a lifeless situation. Think about a time when you were hurting deeply and another person looked at you and said, "I understand what you are feeling, I've been there. I know how hard it is, but you can get through this. It won't be easy, but you will come out stronger than you went in. I'm not letting you do it alone, I'm here for you, and I'll walk with you. I believe in you." You immediately feel a connection to that person. Why? Because our mess brings comfort to others and our beauty brings hope. I want you to feel comfort in knowing you don't have to be perfect. I also want you to find hope. A hope that makes you want to rise up and believe for more. More than you ever believed you could achieve. We only have one chance at this life. Let's make it count. Not by erasing the mess, but by using the mess to illuminate the beauty.

As soon as I got home from my date with Kevin, I dove into Proverbs 31. As I read, I began to cry again. It was like seeing it for the first time. The more I read about Bathsheba I was amazed. There was no indication, allusion, or words that said anything about her being seductive, seducing, or as being an adulterous woman. What I found instead, was how much God loved her! I soon discovered a lesson, a lesson that has changed how I saw God and His involvement in the story of David and Bathsheba. It also caused me to realize again just how important it is to read and research the Bible myself and not only rely on others research and opinions. I had been believing a lie about Bathsheba my whole life. I pondered why I had never questioned the story before. And wondered why I or anyone I knew had never seen it before now. It also jarred a memory that I had forgotten until this moment. Not long before the night at the Indian Restaurant, I had prayed a very specific prayer.

I asked God to show me things in the Bible that I had not seen before. I decided to take God at what He said in Jeremiah 33:3. It says, "Call to Me and I will answer and show you great and unsearchable things you do not know." I thought about what my mom would always say. "Valeri, obligate God. If He tells us something in His word, He means it, and He will do it." So, I called out to God. I asked Him if He would show me some of the hidden treasures, remarkable secrets in His word that I didn't know yet. I even prayed more specifically for Him to show me new things in the old scriptures I had been reading for years. Wow! He did it. And now I was hungry for more.

In the coming chapters we will look directly at the scriptures to see what exactly is said, and just as importantly in this story, what is *not* said about Bathsheba. I look forward to sharing with you all the things I believe God opened my eyes to see.

This was the reason I couldn't stop crying as Kevin explained more of his discovery of the true identity of Bathsheba in the restaurant that night. Somehow with that one sentence "It's Bathsheba" my entire world was rocked to the core. I expected her to be the adulterous woman. The bad girl that brought down the almighty, all wonderful, King David.

Before my brain could fully wrap around how this was against my expectation, the truth was wrapping around my heart and healing it. I didn't just see Bathsheba differently, I began to see myself differently. Could it be possible? Would God actually allow a woman like her to be given the honorable title of "The Virtuous Woman"?

I am not writing this discovery about Bathsheba to be controversial. I am writing it to share the gift I was given that I can't keep to myself. I don't want to cast a shadow of doubt over any pastor, teacher, or godly leader. Everyone is expected to search the scriptures on their own along with learning from our pastors and teachers. I'm challenging you to look for yourself. Look and see what truth you find. However, with truth usually comes resistance. That is okay with me. I am hoping this will be a disruption.

A BEAUTIFUL MESS

Whether you have read the Bible through many times, or you have never read the Bible, this book is for you. We are all starting at the same place. As I mentioned, I grew up in a pastor's home. My grandfather was a pastor. My sisters both married pastors. My uncles were pastors. I married a pastor. I like to joke and call it the pastor mafia. I've been in the "business" my entire life. Oddly, in the eight years I have been researching and talking about this book, (and believe me I have been obsessed with this for eight years), only one person out of everyone I told looked right at me and smiled and said, "Yes, of course I know that is who Bathsheba is." Granted, this guy builds satellites that are currently orbiting in space above us. He is also what you would term a "professional hacker." He teaches our government specialists how to catch criminal hackers. So, it seems fitting he has hacked into the depths of many a Bible story account. However, this is one of the reasons it has taken me so long to write this book. I wanted to dig as much as I could and get as much information as possible to back this incredible finding. The information I have discovered about Bathsheba is so amazing I can't wait to share it with you, so let's get started learning.

~ CHAPTER THREE ~

A Royal Mess

SO WHO IS BATHSHEBA? Is she the virtuous woman? Is she the adulterous woman? Or is she the redeemed adulterous woman? It turns out there is a lot we are told about Bathsheba, but surprisingly after eight years of research I haven't found anything in the Bible or any other historical account that could correctly label her as an adulterous woman. I have found plenty of places where theologians have denigrated Bathsheba through speculation and surmise. The problem with these negative accounts on her character is the lack of substantiated evidence. There is, however, a lot to be gleaned from the story in 2 Samuel, Chapter 11. I would like to now walk through that story with you. I hope your eyes will be opened to see all God wants to show you, including the truth that is hidden in plain sight.

The story of Bathsheba starts with David. 2 Samuel 11:1 says, "In the spring of the year, when kings *normally* go out to war, David sent Joab and the Israelite army to fight the Ammonites. They destroyed the Ammonite army and laid siege to the city of Rabbah. However, David stayed behind in Jerusalem."

It all begins with David being somewhere he did not belong. He belonged out with his men at war. The Bible makes that very clear. It wasn't normal for David to stay behind. He sent Joab instead, and he stayed home. Remember, this is the same David that killed Goliath with a small stone. He was the only Israelite brave enough to fight the giant! David was the leader of the mighty men.

Before becoming king, David had built up a team of men now known as his mighty men. These men were a bunch of misfits and outcasts whom David believed in. David was empathetic to those who were rejected, having known the pain of rejection, and being treated as an outcast in his own family. David built up this team of outcasts who became some of the most loyal, valiant, indomitable fighters in history. This was a true band of brothers. One reason these men were so fiercely loyal to David was because David modeled that loyalty. David was known for being a leader who led by example. He was very committed to fighting alongside his men. So why didn't David go? Why would he send his men out to war while he stayed home lying around? What was going on in his heart? Could it be that pride was beginning to rule the decisions of his heart rather than humility? Did his heart already partner with a plan for some kind of sexual sin? Is that why he stayed back while all his men went off to fight the war? One thing we can say for certain, David was acting very different. He was acting different from any other account of him in the Bible up to this point.

2 Samuel 11:2 continues, "Late one afternoon, after his midday rest, David got out of bed and was walking on the rooftop of the palace. As he looked out over the city, he noticed a woman of unusual beauty taking a bath. He sent someone to find out who she was, and he was told, "She is Bathsheba, the daughter of Eliam and the wife of Uriah the Hittite."

First red flag, he was waking up late in the afternoon, after his midday rest? Why was he laying around and sleeping so much? Was he tired? Had he become lazy? Had he begun to identify more with his entitlement as king, than with his responsibility? His men were at war fighting – possibly dying – and he was content to leisurely rest and roam, looking in the direction of the home of one of his closest friends and loyal mighty men, Uriah.

What happened to the David of Psalm 5:3 who

penned, "In the morning, Lord, You hear my voice; In the morning I lay my requests before You and wait with expectation." Or what about the David in Psalm 119:147-148, "I rise before dawn and cry for help; I wait for Your words. My eyes anticipate the night watches, that I may meditate on Your word." I'll give him the benefit of the doubt. Maybe he did get up early that day. Maybe he was just taking a late afternoon nap. However, from the outcome of this day, it doesn't seem like he was doing a lot of praying that morning.

Proverbs 24:33-34 was written by David's son Solomon and it says, "A little sleep, a little slumber, a little folding of the hands to rest – then your poverty will come *as* a robber, and your *want* like an armed man." David's poverty may not have been material poverty, it might have been poverty of the heart. Any area in his heart that had not been fully healed and filled by God. We all have a void that at some point we are going to need filled. If we don't allow God to fill our poverty of heart, the enemy will be happy to offer a counterfeit. As with David, the counterfeit is intended to destroy our heart. We see David warning his son of this very thing in the following scripture, "Guard your heart above all else, for it determines the course of your life" (Proverbs 4:23 NLT). The title of this chapter in Proverbs says, "A father's wise advice." Solomon, the son of David, and Bathsheba is the author of the book of Proverbs.

Now, you may be picturing the famous paintings you've seen that depict this event. The ones where the artist makes it look like Bathsheba is doing a strip-tease. Or, Rembrandt's famous painting of her sitting naked holding the letter from David. Maybe like me you have a picture formed in your mind made up from all the Sundays growing up in Sunday school and hearing the teacher talk about the bad woman who wasn't being modest. The naughty woman that caused the king after God's heart to sin. The countless sermons I heard growing up about the woman I never wanted to be. The one that caused a good man to fall into sin.

I want to point out another discrepancy in the version of this story that has somehow become a main theme of the account. I have always pictured Bathsheba out on her rooftop in the afternoon sun, naked and bathing seductively for David to watch. Yet, there is not one version of the Bible I have found that has ever mentioned Bathsheba on her rooftop. David was on his rooftop, and from his rooftop he saw a woman bathing. I'm not saying this means she wasn't on her rooftop, I am just highlighting the fact the Bible does not say she was on a rooftop, nor do the scriptures say where she was bathing. She could have been in the courtyard of her rooftop, as there was no indoor plumbing in those days. Contrary to the versions of this story I was told, nowhere in the scriptures does it mention anything about Bathsheba being naked. Somehow we've contrived a complete fallacy in the depiction of Bathsheba at her bath. From Sunday School to famous artistic depictions, we have a very distinct picture of what Bathsheba was presumably doing that evening. Somehow she has been accused of being on her rooftop bathing fully naked with intention of capturing the attention of the king. Another thing to keep in mind is that bathing in those days was different than how we consider bathing today. The art we see depicting bathing in those days usually shows a person partially nude with a cloth covering part of their body. Getting water to the designated bathing area required pitchers of water brought from wells or possibly caught from rainfall. It was common to refer to bathing as the washing of feet and hands. Let's review the details we are given about Bathsheba from scripture again. Using only scripture, we will see how the preconceived depiction of Bathsheba bathing seductively for David while naked on a rooftop is fallacy. Going back to 2 Samuel 11:2 we will read the account from David's perspective, "Late one afternoon, after his midday rest, David got out of bed and was walking on the rooftop of the palace. As he looked out over the city, he noticed a woman of unusual beauty taking a bath."

I think it is important to look at these facts from scripture and compare them to the false perception that has made its way through history, unfairly marring the true character and identity of Bathsheba. It makes the picture in my mind seem a bit ridiculous. The palace was significantly higher than all the surrounding homes giving David a bird's eye view from his rooftop. Considering that those surrounding homes most likely were occupied by people the king could trust. These people would not be strangers to David. In fact, three of the homes most likely belonged to Bathsheba's family. Bathsheba's husband Uriah, and her father, Eliam (also known as Ammiel) were both mighty men in David's army. Bathsheba's grandfather Ahithophel, was the chief counselor and most trusted advisor to David. Scripture tells us Ahithophel ranked above even the priests (1 Chronicles 27:33, 34). The Bible says, "Absalom followed Ahithophel's advice, just as David had done. For every word Ahithophel spoke seemed as wise as though it had come directly from the mouth of God" (2 Samuel 16:23 NLT). Bathsheba was related to three of David's most honorable military leaders. It seems odd to me that David had no idea who he was looking at. After looking at these facts about Bathsheba, it seems improbable that David had never met Bathsheba before. The closest men to her in her life were some of the closest and most trusted men in David's life. Another thing we have to take into consideration is David's admiration of beautiful women. Bathsheba was very beautiful. The scripture made that clear when it highlighted David noticing a woman of unusual beauty taking a bath. He had multiple wives and many concubines, he had become quite the connoisseur of beautiful women. With this in mind, it seems he would have at least taken notice of Uriah's beautiful wife. Uriah was one of David's closest friends, one in his elite group of trusted mighty men. He was a commander of a division, renowned for his exploits and service to the king. Uriah was a trench buddy who fought alongside David long before David was king. He wasn't some distant acquaintance of David. The Bible does not explicitly say David knew Bathsheba. Yet, given the exploits of her family's rich military pedigree and her unusual beauty, the probability of David at least knowing of Bathsheba seems far more likely than not. The reason there is no more mention beyond this information could be that some things don't require further explanation. They require common sense.

When David asks who this woman is, the answer from the servant comes threaded with a familiar tone "It's Bathsheba, Eliam's daughter, Uriah's wife."

It seems the servant assumed David knew exactly who he was talking about. This is where we see a different David than we're used to seeing in the Bible. "Then David sent messengers to get her, and when she came to the palace, he slept with her. (She had just completed her purification rites after having her menstrual period). Then she returned home." Wow! That was fast. David didn't take a second to let that information sink in. He wanted her. That is all he was focused on. And he got her. And then he sent her home.

Jesus says in Matthew 5:28, "But I tell you that anyone who looks at a woman lustfully has already committed adultery with her in his heart." I wonder how far he had allowed himself to entertain lustful thoughts previous to this one moment. Having six wives and many concubines leads me to think he may have had a problem with sexual addiction or lust. Even though it was acceptable in the culture of that time, God never said concubines were permitted for a man to have. However, this might have been part of what started to lead David's heart to commit adultery. I will even take my liberties here and speculate a little. It seems there could be a good chance this was not the first time David had taken this evening stroll along the rooftop, perhaps he found just what he was looking for. Or, the enemy of his soul knew the condition of his heart, and this was a perfect time to pounce.

This can be a teaching moment for all of us! We may have a heart that loves God and desires to please Him, yet, if we are not careful, we too can become complacent and careless with what we allow our eyes to see, our ears to hear, our minds to think. Next thing we know, we have fallen into sin that hurts us and brings destruction into our life and the lives around us. The most dangerous place is in our mind. The area we become too complacent in is our thought life. Our mind is our freewill. Our will comes from our heart. This is why we must guard our heart. The mind is the guard over our heart. "For as a man thinks in his heart, so is he" (Proverbs 23:7 NKJV). This scripture from the book of Proverbs, was penned by David and Bathsheba's son Solomon. Most likely what his mother taught him.

What we think is ultimately what we do. The first place the enemy goes is for your mind. He knows that if he can get you into agreement with his suggestions, you will fall. Our thoughts alone are not sin. We will all think crazy things. It is what we do with the thought that determines whether or not we sin. Just because a lustful thought goes through your mind, does not immediately translate to sin. It is what you decide to do with the thought that determines the outcome. We are to take the thought captive as the Bible instructs us to do, "Casting down imaginations, and every high thing that is exalted against the knowledge of God, and bringing every thought into captivity to the obedience of Christ" (2 Corinthians 10:5 AKJV).

Our mind is powerful. We have to choose what we come into agreement with carefully. The enemy knows if we get into agreement with his suggestions in our mind, he will gain authority over it. If we get into agreement with him, we take his hand and go with him on the path he thinks is best for us. He likes to start by walking us backwards. He will take you on a quick revisit to your past. If you are a Christian, that is a very dangerous trip. We are not allowed back there once Jesus covers it. You see, our past is different once it is covered by the blood of Jesus. So, if you decide to go back there with the enemy, you are now entering a false version of your past. It will be Satan's version. His version of your past will drench your heart in shame, regret, fear, anger, hopelessness, condemnation, and insecurity. He will convince you on that journey that you are beyond hope. You already blew it so bad it doesn't matter what you do now. It does matter. It matters a lot. It matters so much that Jesus will never take you down that path. Jesus forgets *your* past. Once you give it to Him, He rewrites your story in His redeeming blood. Therefore, your past can now bring hope to others. Your past serves only as a reminder of His amazing grace. Your past is only there to remind you of what He did for you on the cross to cover it all in His blood. We must be ready to cast down those thoughts with truth. You and I are not the same person we were before giving our heart to Jesus.

David took the bait. He allowed his heart to get into agreement with the enemy. The rest we see is history. Also, as we see with the story of David and Bathsheba, it never just affects you. It affects everyone around you. David's one decision affected so many people.

Bathsheba probably didn't think David was at the palace and certainly not walking around on his rooftop while all the men were off to war. Her husband, father, and most likely her grandfather were all gone. In verse four it says, "then David sent messengers to get her." This is not a phone call, or an invitation in the mail. This is a group of powerful men, showing up at your door while your husband is off at war. They tell you the king wants to see you immediately. Let's keep in mind, she grew up in a military family. She is married to one of David's mighty men. This woman knew when summoned by the king, you went. You did not have any say in the matter. If you refused, you could be killed. There was no question of whether or not she could decline.

I've wondered if in that moment of hearing she was summoned by the king, knowing that he wanted to see her immediately, if fear shot through her. I wonder if she was thinking her husband had been badly wounded or even killed. Or could it possibly be her father, or grandfather? Who knows? We also certainly cannot assume that she had any indication that David wanted to have sex with her.

I wonder what it must have been like to be in Bathsheba's shoes. Here she is, summoned by the king. King David, the strong, valiant, mighty, and handsome King David. He was the man after God's own heart. She has heard how he defeated many armies and how he led the mighty men to victory for God! So, she goes when he summons her, and soon she finds out that he is filled with lust for her! The verse continues, "and when she came to the palace, *he* slept with her." The verse is clear that David is the initiator. Now, no one, including me, wants to call the wonderful King David a rapist. However, I don't want to call him a murderer either. Or an adulterer who took one of his best friend's wife. I am not calling him a rapist.

However, I do think we need to look at what the Bible is saying and see who is being highlighted for the act. He called her, she came, and David initiated the act that ultimately resulted in sin. Bathsheba was probably too fearful to resist. In the culture of that day, women did not have a voice, they had no say in what they would or would not do, especially if it was the king wanting something. They were treated more like property. They were not considered equal.

God did not approve of this cultural ideal, no more than He agrees with any other thing going on in our culture that is dishonoring. But that was the culture of the time. There was no mention here of Bathsheba saying or doing anything. It just tells us what David did. I think what it says, is enough. Bathsheba didn't have a voice at this point. David was the one who had the power. He was calling the shots.

Verse four continues, "She had just completed the purification rites after having her menstrual period." This is a very important part to this verse. Yet, it has always seemed weird to me. Why was that placed there? In other translations of the Bible it has this particular verse in parenthesis. Another example is from the New International Version. ("Now, she was purifying herself from her monthly uncleanness.") In the King James Version it says, "Then David sent messengers, and took her; and she came to him, and he lay with her, for she was cleansed from her impurity; and she returned to her house." It is telling us that she was already cleansed before he lay with her. In those days in that culture a woman was considered unclean during her menstrual period. Men were not to have sexual relations with a woman during her period and for up to seven days after. The woman performed this act up to seven days after the last day of their menstrual period. The information added here would not seem strange to a person from that culture and time. It also debunks the theory that Bathsheba was purifying herself after having sex with David. It also tells us she wasn't pregnant with Uriah's child before David slept with her.

~ CHAPTER FOUR ~

A Man after God's Own Heart

Now I HAVE TO pause here and make something clear before going any further. I do not want to vilify David. David was a good man, who did a lot of good. He was known for his integrity and upright character. He was known as a man after God's own heart. However, he was just a man. He was not God. He came from an incredible mess, growing up. Yes, he fought and killed lions and bears while protecting the sheep under his care. He killed the powerful giant Goliath and led Israel to victory over the Philistine army. But David was also in a continual battle with another giant in his life - the giant stronghold of rejection. He talks openly about it in the book of Psalms. He was an outcast in his own family. He wasn't even treated as a son. He was treated as a servant. Although his father, Jesse, was a farmer and sheep breeder, they came from a successful and respected family. Many scholars and commentaries say in families like the one David came from, sons were not usually the ones sent out to care for the sheep. That was the job of a servant. Keep in mind, Jesse was the grandson of Boaz and Ruth. Boaz was a very wealthy landowner in Bethlehem. Obed the son of Boaz and Ruth, father of Jesse, would have been the sole heir of all the wealth of Boaz. Jesse was often referred to as Jesse the Bethlehemite. A Bethlehemite would be considered a native inhabitant of Bethlehem.

Although David was sent out to tend the sheep, it was not because of anything David did wrong. He talks about how he had to pay for sins that he did not commit. His parents had problems. His father was well known in the temple as a godly man. Yet, David was treated by Jesse as an outcast. The Bible clearly says David, son of Jesse. But something happened. Some speculate that David's mother sinned and committed adultery. Other accounts suggest Jesse stepped out of the marriage and slept with another woman. In that culture, it seems less probable that it was David's mother that sinned because in that culture the consequence of a woman caught in the sin of adultery was punishable by death. And most importantly, the Bible calls David, the son of Jesse. The point I want to highlight is this: generational sin is very real. It passes down just the same as generational blessings. David was carrying not only the generational sin of his parents undealt with adultery, he was carrying the stronghold of rejection in his heart. I don't claim to know all the facts concerning David's parents or upbringing, but it is something I would encourage you to consider.

For a while I was having a hard time not being angry with David. I was angry that David would keep the title, "a man after God's own heart" (1 Samuel 13:14), even after the mess he created with Bathsheba and the devastation he brought to her life. As well as, the evil of stealing your loyal friend and soldier's wife, sleeping with her, and then having him killed to cover it up. I was angry that the culture did not give women a place to speak up, or speak back to a king.

I also began to insert my own disappointments into this story. It started to seem more like the, "Here we go again, another so-called Christian man can't seem to control his lust." If I were honest, I had some disappointment and anger of my own that was being triggered. I started asking God about it. At first I just kept it in my heart. Then I realized this could keep me from being able to write this book because the last thing I could do was write a book and totally vilify one of the most beloved and famous men in the Bible! Especially one that God highlighted and loved so much. So, I finally had it out with God. I got real with God.

"God!" I said, "I don't understand how you allowed David to carry the most honorable title of "A man after your own heart." This guy was a jerk. Yes he did do some incredible things, and seemed to be a great guy before this account. But he clearly used his power over innocent people and hurt and killed them. What is that all about? Don't you care that people will read into this and think you are saying that is who you are? So this is what a man after God's own heart looks and acts like? Wow!" I went on from there, "Also, since I'm just going for it, why God, why would you let a man after your own heart have multiple wives and concubines?" To be honest, that had always bothered me! I was never able to wrap my head around it. It was wrong! Period! In my opinion and after doing my own research on it, concubines were nothing more than modern day sex slaves. Maybe they were given better living conditions. Maybe they weren't treated as brutally as what we know as sex trafficking today. I'm sure they were brainwashed to believe that somehow it was honorable to be "chosen" to be a concubine of the king. However, these were women. Human beings. I'm sure they wouldn't choose to be one of the hundreds of women to be at the beck and call of the "needy" king. I'll never forget what I felt God say to me so clearly. He said, "When did I ever say it was okay? Where do you see in scripture I ever said it was okay?" I guess I didn't think of it that way. God didn't ever say it was okay that David had concubines. He also never said it was okay to have multiple wives. There is clear instruction from God in Deuteronomy 17:17 regarding what is acceptable behavior for kings. It says "A king must not take for himself many wives, or his heart will be led astray." In fact, as the story goes on, we will see that this is when David's heart began to change.

Whenever we begin to convince ourselves that doing something directly against God's word is somehow okay we will begin to change. That is when we take the guard away from our heart. That is how pride gets in. This is why it is so important, above all else, to guard our heart because it truly is the wellspring of our soul. The tender hearted David is beginning to harden his heart to God. I believe this was what ushered in the devastation in his life. Our choices have consequences. We see this with David. God didn't need to say anything else to David. David knew what God said about this. David loved the law of the Lord. He was the one that said he meditated on it day and night. It seems David was starting to see himself more as a king, instead of keeping his eyes on the one who made him king.

If God said David was a man after His heart, I felt as though God was putting a stamp of approval on his sin, too. Or at least looking the other way. I guess I was thinking David had to be perfect in order to hold that title. I was putting a standard on David that none of us could measure up to. Well, come on, Joseph would be a better candidate than David though, right? Why David? I guess there are a lot of better candidates than me out there that should be writing this book. Thankfully, God doesn't judge the way we judge. God sees our heart, and He is the only one that matters. We only see the outward expression of what is in the heart.

Perhaps God saw the rejected young boy. In Psalm 69 we hear the heart of David that is hurting because of rejection. Many Biblical Scholars say Psalm 69 is a Messianic prophecy of Jesus and His suffering for us on the cross. After studying the Bible, I see this as God using David and his suffering to pen these descriptions so well. It also shows another picture of how David was a man after God's own heart. He is describing the heart of Jesus and His sufferings as He was going to the cross – dying on the cross. A description of one who was being mocked and pushed around. One that longed to be at the table with his brothers, but instead was made to sit in a corner in the other room. Jewish tradition tells us that David was treated terribly. He was treated as an outcast in his family. It says he was punished because of the sin of his conception.

He was a boy who felt so humiliated when he passed by the leaders at the city gate who would call him deplorable names. A boy who carried a weight too heavy to bear, and sins that weren't his to carry. What do you do when you're handed the baggage of your parents? The baggage that just keeps getting wrapped up so beautifully and ever so gingerly placed into the suitcases of the next generation. Carrying on and passing down from generation to generation. Each time it is passed there is a little more added. We wonder why things are so messy? That is why. If we don't stop the baggage train in our family, who will?

If I can pass on one thing to you, it would be this: let God in when you're mad and when you're sad, no matter what you are going through. He really can handle it and He really does get it. I think we cheat God out of having a say in our relationship with Him. We do all the talking. We automatically blame Him for everything, yet we rarely stop to ask Him what He has to say about anything. I am so glad I let God in on this. One thing I have learned as I have gotten closer to God is He always has something to say.

He will always answer if we ask Him to. It helped me a lot when God showed me His heart on this. It also gave me a new and fresh understanding on why David was called, "A man after God's own heart." David was after God's heart. He cried out to God. He rejoiced with God, he complained to God. He even asked God to wipe out his enemies. This was a man who trusted God. He poured his heart out to God's heart. He had developed a relationship with God as a young boy, when God was the only person he had to rely on. David's lonely years were a gift. He would never have known God the way he did without those lonely years out in the sheep pen. However, that messy pen was preparing this future king for the palace. As I continued to question my own expectations, I realized God was upset that David did this, and so upset, He called him out for it!

It would be easy for any of us to categorize David with other men that have disappointed us. For some of you, this hits very close to home. Some of you might have had a man that everyone held in highest esteem, seemingly even God, deeply hurt or disappoint you. I hope that as you begin to see David more as a real person, with real pain and struggles just like all of us, it will help you find the strength to forgive and to allow God heal your broken heart. I also hope you will begin to see God in a new and fresh way. The heart of God that cares deeply about your hurt and pain. He wants to protect your heart just as we will see He did with Bathsheba. David was a very good man who had a problem. Yes, at first, he had a heart that was soft towards God, but then as time went on, he started justifying things. Or, he just didn't deal with the things in his heart that eventually became bigger than he could manage. Just because we love God and desire to live for Him, we still have to choose to walk in honesty and purity before Him. Whatever the case may be, through this journey, I learned something from God. I learned I don't see the whole picture. Only God does. That is why we are commanded not to judge. We don't have the ability to judge fairly.

Let's continue with verses 5-13, "Later, when Bathsheba discovered that she was pregnant, she sent David a message, saying, 'I'm Pregnant.' Then David sent word to Joab, 'Send me Uriah the Hittite.' So Joab sent Uriah to David. When Uriah came to him, David asked concerning the welfare of Joab and the people and the state of the war. Then David said to Uriah, 'Go down to your house, and wash your feet.' And Uriah went out of the king's house, and a present from the king was sent out after him. But Uriah slept at the door of the king's house with all the servants of his lord, and did not go down to his house. Now when they told David, saying, 'Uriah did not go down to his house,' David said to Uriah, 'Have you not come from a journey? Why did you not go down to your house?' Uriah said to David, 'The ark and Israel and Judah are staying in temporary shelters, and my lord Joab and the servants of my lord are camping in the open field. Shall I then go to my house to eat and to drink and to lie with my wife? By your life and the life of your soul, I will not do this thing.' Then David said to Uriah, 'Stay here today also, and tomorrow I will let you go.' So Uriah remained in Jerusalem that day and the next. Now David called him, and he ate and drank before him, and he made him drunk; and in the evening, he went out to lie on his bed with his lord's servants, but he did not go down to his house."

We are seeing David do things from a heart that seems to be much less tuned to God. This looks more like someone who doesn't really care about what God thinks. Where is the David that talked to God about everything? The tender-hearted David, that felt bad when he sinned? The David that would lament before God and make it right. I don't think David changed all of a sudden from that man after God's heart to a man capable of such detestable behavior. This was a progression. I started to wonder when he took his first concubine, then he got another - could it possibly have been a trap he was falling into that was filling a need? Was it feeding a hunger that had been in him for a long time? The hunger to be wanted, the need for intimacy and the desire to quiet the lion of rejection.

If we're not careful we can all find ourselves using something else to fill the voids in our hearts instead of going to God. God knew the big picture. God was looking at David's heart. However, God was also looking very intently after Bathsheba's heart as well.

I wonder if Uriah knew that David was up to something. His men had to see the change in David. These were the people closest to David. Were they already a bit disgusted with how he had been acting? It seems if David was jumping to the decisions alone in this story and as fast as he was, there was an obvious problem going on with him. It seems David was drinking pretty heavily as well for it to be normal for him to have Uriah come for dinner in hopes to get him drunk. That doesn't sound like the David I read about in the Psalms. His heart was different. I'm sure Uriah was on to David's strange behavior. He had to wonder what he was doing. Or, maybe he had a clue. Uriah calls attention to David's behavior when he questions how David would want him to go home and eat and drink and sleep with his wife when his brothers were out on the line, risking their lives. In this passage, the soft-hearted David was not there. David thought if he could manipulate Uriah to sleep with Bathsheba, he would be off the hook, and everyone would think the pregnancy was legitimate, but maybe Uriah saw through it.

In 2 Samuel 11:14-15, we see the ugliness in David's heart as he becomes more determined to hide his mess. He does not confess or ask for forgiveness. If he had, many people may have been spared. Instead, "In the morning David wrote a letter to Joab and sent it by the hand of Uriah. He had written in the letter, saying, "Place Uriah in the front line of the fiercest battle and withdraw from him, so that he may be struck down and die."

David broke the commandments of God when he slept with Bathsheba. He coveted his neighbor's wife, and then committed adultery with her. In an attempt to cover up his sin, he lies. And in an attempt to cover his lies, he murders. Hiding always leads to more sin and a bigger mess, not less. Imagine what Joab thought in that moment! David had been overcome with something evil, and he was not the same guy. How could he send Uriah back to the battle carrying his own death sentence in his bag. He delivered his own death sentence to Joab. You don't think Joab was thinking the same thing? Who does this? Where did David go? This was unbelievable. I'm sure Joab cared about Uriah. It had to be one of the hardest things he ever did in his life. Essentially, David was asking Joab to kill Uriah. He asked Joab to make the call. I don't think Joab ever looked at David the same again. How could he?

Verses 16-21 say, "So it was as Joab kept watch on the city, that he put Uriah at the place where he knew there were valiant men. The men of the city went out and fought against Joab, and some of the people among David's servants fell; and Uriah the Hittite also died. Then Joab sent and reported to David all the events of the war. He charged the messenger, saying, "When you have finished telling all the events of the war to the king, and if it happens that the king's wrath rises and he says to you, 'Why did you go so near to the city to fight? Did you not know that they would shoot from the wall? Who struck down Abimelech the son of Jerubbesheth? Did not a woman throw an upper millstone on him from the wall so that he died at Thebez? Why did you go so near the wall?'—then you shall say, 'Your servant Uriah the Hittite is dead also." This is incredible. David sinned and then he tried to hide it. The consequence of hiding it was the murder of Uriah and several other men.

In verses 22-25, the servant tells all this to David, and verses 26-27 say, "Now when the wife of Uriah heard that Uriah her husband was dead, she mourned for her husband. When the time of mourning was over, David sent and brought her to his house and she became his wife; then she bore him a son. But the thing that David had done was evil in the sight of the Lord."

Notice Bathsheba is not called by her name, she is called, the wife of Uriah. God is making it clear: she was not David's. She belonged to Uriah. God also intentionally tells us Bathsheba's response to the news of her husband's death. She did what any wife would do over a husband she loved, she mourned for her husband. When the period of mourning was over, David sent for her again. This time to become one of his many wives.

David already had six wives and many concubines (2 Samuel 5:13). He had many women and he wanted her too. God did not condone this. God clarifies the fault and the wrongdoing in 2 Samuel 11:27, "The thing that David had done was evil in the sight of the Lord." This is God's word! It is God's assessment of the situation. It does not say, David and Bathsheba had done evil. It just speaks of what David did in the sight of the Lord.

Think about Bathsheba! She was dealing with the ultimate shame of becoming pregnant when her husband was off to war. The king was the father of her baby. She had been stripped of everything she called her life. She is mourning the death of her husband. She can't call her godly, wise grandfather for help and advice or her father for help. In that culture she could be killed. Instead, she is once again summoned by the king. Think of it through her eyes. Here's the king that took advantage of you, killed your husband, and now wants you as his seventh wife. Imagine how desolate her heart felt. She was probably afraid of David. He wasn't the kind-hearted king she had heard of. He was capable of anything. Yet she had no choice, but to go again when summoned by the king. This time she never returned home. It was the beginning of a whole new life. We will now begin to see this familiar story from the perspective of Bathsheba. Seeing the palace, David, and the life she is just beginning, through her eyes.

~ CHAPTER FIVE ~

Prisoner in the Palace

BATHSHEBA IS NOW LIVING in the palace as the seventh wife of King David. No doubt there is much speculation and gossip flying around regarding her. She saw the looks and heard the whispers when she entered a room. She had been given a new title, an honorable title, as the new wife of the king. Although this was not the title she was looking for, in that day it was custom to kill a woman caught in adultery, there was no punishment to the man. God made a way for Bathsheba. Instead of being killed, Bathsheba is brought into the palace and given a position of honor as David's wife.

I can't help but think how lonely she must have felt. She is the new wife of the king. One of seven women who hold the exact same title. Her husband is gone. Her father, and her grandfather are two of

David's right hand men. How could she have a normal relationship with her father or grandfather? It must have been so scary. David was not the tender-hearted king he once was, if he was capable of all he had just done. What else was he capable of? Remember, he hadn't repented. From all we see to this point, it didn't look like he was planning on repenting. He was just moving on as if nothing had happened. He married Bathsheba and brought her to the palace to be his wife. All of a sudden, you don't have anyone to protect you. You've gone from being married to a mighty warrior, and having a father who was a mighty warrior, to not being able to call on anyone for help. She couldn't talk to her grandfather and ask for his wisdom. She couldn't ask her dad to rescue her. These were his most loyal men, they had to support the king. It was their duty. She had to wait on God to rescue her. He was her only hope.

She did have one bright spot in the midst of everything. She had her baby. Regardless of the circumstances that led to her becoming pregnant, she had a light at the end of all this darkness. This precious baby that she could pour her heart into. She would focus on the joy God gave her in that baby to fill the void of all the loss and pain, while she waited on God to bring her vindication. And God brought Nathan. Nathan was a prophet of God. He was also a friend and trusted advisor of David. David highly respected Nathan because he knew he was a man of God.

2 Samuel 12 says, "So the Lord sent Nathan the prophet to tell David this story: "There were two men in a certain town. One was rich, and one was poor. The rich man owned a great many sheep and cattle. The poor man owned nothing but one little lamb he had bought. He raised that little lamb, and it grew up with his children. It ate from the man's own plate and drank from his cup. He cuddled it in his arms like a baby daughter. One day a guest arrived at the home of the rich man. But instead of killing an animal from his own flock or herd, he took the poor man's lamb and killed it and prepared it for his guest." David was furious. "As surely as the Lord lives," he vowed, "Any man who would do such a thing deserves to die! He must repay four lambs to the poor man for the one he stole and for having no pity."

Then Nathan said to David, "You are that man! The Lord, the God of Israel, says: I anointed you king of Israel and saved you from the power of Saul. I gave you your master's house and his wives and the kingdoms of Israel and Judah. And if that had not been enough, I would have given you much, much more. Why, then, have you despised the word of the Lord and done this horrible deed? For you have murdered Uriah the Hittite with the sword of the

Ammonites and stolen his wife. From this time on, your family will live by the sword because you have despised me by taking Uriah's wife to be your own."

"This is what the Lord says: Because of what you have done, I will cause your own household to rebel against you. I will give your wives to another man before your very eyes, and he will go to bed with them in public view. You did it secretly, but I will make this happen to you openly in the sight of all Israel" (NLT).

Let's look at this rebuke from Nathan with a fresh set of lenses. Many of us with church background have read this more times than we could count. Even those of you who haven't been in church, I bet it's safe to assume you have at least heard about it. Regardless of your background, this is when we all land on the same playing field. This is the game changer.

Let's look at the first thing Nathan the prophet went after. He went after the rich man (David) who stole from the poor man (Uriah). Nathan goes on to describe in detail what the rich man stole from the poor man. He tells David how the rich man owned a great many cattle and sheep. But the poor man owned nothing but one little lamb. Nathan goes on to describe in detail about this little lamb of the poor man. He talks about how he loved this lamb. How he fed the lamb at his table, how he cuddled this lamb in his arms like a baby daughter. Nathan goes on to describe a day in which a guest arrived at the rich man's house. Instead of killing an animal from his own flock he took the lamb from the poor man, killed it, and prepared it for his hungry guest.

Who is the lamb in this parable? It is Bathsheba. We see the poor man is Uriah. You would think God would go after David for killing Uriah since he is the person David actually killed. Instead, God goes right after Bathsheba being stolen from Uriah and David killing her to serve to his hungry guest that had come to town.

Bathsheba is the only person in the Bible that is referred to as a lamb besides Jesus. The actual translation for the lamb Nathan is referring to is a ewe. The definition of a ewe is a grown female sheep. She is referenced as a grown female lamb. Why is Jesus called the lamb that was slain for our sins? Because a lamb is used to describe innocence. Without sin. God is very angry about what David did to Bathsheba. He makes that crystal clear. He also makes sure we all see her as he sees her. She was dearly loved by her husband. She was purchased, meaning she belonged to Uriah as his wife. She was precious to him. He cuddled her in his arms. She was stolen from him, and killed to serve a hungry guest.

We finally see the heart of David being awakened. The heart for justice. It says he was furious! He says any man that would do such a thing should die. He should have to give four lambs to the poor man for the one he stole for having no pity! And then Nathan lowered the boom! David, you are that man! Wow.

David was still blind to his sin, even as Nathan was describing it with great detail. His heart had grown cold to the spirit of God. However, God knew just how to get his attention. God wasn't going to let Bathsheba pay for this sin. God is amazing at taking care of us if we just get out of His way.

God showed me another huge part of this rebuke that I had never noticed. It hit me like a ton of bricks. Maybe because I studied addiction, and have counseled many people with this problem. What God showed me was paramount to this entire story.

One night as I was going over this rebuke I felt this part just jump off the page. I felt like God whispered the question in my spirit, "who is the hungry guest Valeri?" I about fell out of my seat. The hungry guest was lust. However, this was a different kind of lust. You see, David had plenty of women to satisfy any desire he would ever dream up. So why didn't he just call one of his many women to satisfy him that evening? In addiction when the hungry guest comes to town, that guest isn't leaving until it is fed.

You see, addiction is something that is repeated over and over. In order for there to be satisfaction you have to have more of whatever it is you're wanting. Unfortunately, with sexual addiction like any other addiction, it takes more and more to satisfy the desire. It may start with looking at pictures on social media. It grows to a little more risky and inappropriate content. Once you lose the adrenaline rush from that level, you have to go to the next level to get the rush. It eventually leads to places one would never have dreamt they would go. The hungry guest shows up and it won't be satisfied until it is fed. This is why child pornography and sex trafficking are even tolerated. Why would anyone want to look at that kind of garbage? Even worse, be a participant in that kind of abuse? It is the same reason a CEO of a successful company who once had a view of the city from their skyscraper office becomes a drug addict, lying strung out on the street below. Or the reason a marriage is torn apart because the spouse that is addicted can't get rid of the hungry guest that keeps showing up. You will always need more drugs, more alcohol, more food, more money, more anger, more applause, more likes on social media, more plastic surgery, more admiration, and more notoriety. You will need more of whatever it is that has your heart, the void in your heart that is perpetually hungry. Why? Because lust is never satisfied.

David began to convince himself that having

multiple wives and concubines was okay. Why did he even entertain that? Well, it was a common thing in that culture at that time. Not for the godly, but it was acceptable, even admired, in high status circles. So, it probably started with one, then two, and he began to justify it with the fact that everyone did it. It wasn't that big of a deal. It was legal. It wasn't like he didn't purchase them. He probably told himself he was helping them by giving them a better life. He was feeding something that felt good at the time. No one gets into addiction seeking pleasure, they get into addiction to avoid pain. "Above all else, guard your heart, for everything you do flows from it" (Proverbs 4:23 NIV).

Although God cared about David, He was very displeased and angry at what David did. David had crossed the line. He hurt God's daughter. His precious lamb. He loved her, He cherished her, He saw what David did. He wanted Bathsheba to know He saw her crushed spirit and how she was robbed of everything good in her life. She was not killed physically. Instead, David crushed her spirit; he broke her heart and killed everything that brought her joy and hope. He did all of this to satisfy his lust. Wow!

Anyone who is reading this right now and has been abused or hurt to the point of feeling like Bathsheba, I want you to know God is sending you a message through this story as well. He is angry at what happened to you. He is very displeased with whomever hurt you. He also wants you to know He hasn't forgotten. He will make your wrongs right. Let Him in. Do what Bathsheba did, as hard as it must have been for her, in the face of total hopelessness, she waited for God. He came through for her, and He wants you to know, He is coming for you.

This is when I began to realize how precious Bathsheba really was. She was nothing like the woman I had made her out to be in my mind. How did she become so misunderstood? Why would something this obvious be overlooked? I think many of us can relate to that feeling though. Some of you reading this right now feel like you have been completely overlooked and so wrongly taken advantage of. How could anyone do what they have done to you and get by with it? Well I assure you, they haven't gotten away with anything. God promises us that He will vindicate us. He will fight for us. He will make our mess into something beautiful. All you have to do is hand it over to Him, allow Him to bring His beauty into your mess.

Maybe you relate more to David and this is making you feel even worse than you already felt about yourself. I want to speak to you very clearly. God loves you! His heart is breaking seeing you in the pain and hopeless cycle the enemy has convinced you that you deserve. He wants to fill the void in your heart with His unconditional love. He wants to restore to you the years that have been stolen. God sees you redeemed and covered in His precious blood. You look up to Him through your mess and shame. However, He is looking over you and all He sees is His robe of righteousness covering your shame. He paid the ultimate price so you could be covered. You could be free. You can begin again. It is never too late for a fresh start. Today is the day of salvation. David wrote, "For you created my inmost being; you knit me together in my mother's womb. I praise you because I am fearfully and wonderfully made" (Psalm 139:13-14 NIV). He made you. He knew if you would allow Him to be your strength, and your father, you would accomplish all the things He put in you to accomplish on this earth. You come *from* God, He sent you *through* your parents. No one else can do what He made you to do. He kissed you and placed a piece of eternity in your heart so you'd always long to come back to Him. You are His, and He adores you. Allow Him to make something beautiful out of your mess. Decide that today is when you are going to stop filling the voids of your heart with destructive things. Allow Him into your mess, confess what you've done wrong to God and to the ones you've hurt. Allow God to heal you and those you have hurt. Then choose to walk a different path.

The difference between how God handles things and how we think He should handle them is the place we can get stuck. The reason is, He sees the details we can't see. He saw the root of where this evil was coming from with David. He didn't see David as evil, He saw that evil had gotten to David. David had opened a door to his heart and the enemy rushed in. You see, the enemy tries to get us as soon as he can. When we are young, he is after our heart. If he can crush your heart, he can rule your mind. Our mind is the passageway to our heart. "As a man thinks in his heart, so is he" (Proverbs 27:4 KJV).

David had become comfortable. He was successful, rich, and the beloved king of Israel. He wasn't in the lonely shepherd's pen, or running for his life from Saul. He wasn't being treated as an outcast anymore, he was being treated as the most important, most loved and respected man in all of Israel. So why now? Why now would he resort to this kind of sin? The answer is simple. We usually don't work as hard to guard our heart when everything is going great. It's easy to let our guard down and relax. Often, we lose the incentive to keep ourselves as sharp, and disciplined. We begin to get comfortable in our success. We begin to think we are entitled to it. We forget so quickly how we got to the wonderful place we are at. We get less diligent about guarding our heart and our mind. The enemy loves it when we start getting comfortable.

This royal position David was enjoying was feeding a void in his heart. Whenever we begin to let other things besides God fill the voids in our heart, we are headed down a slippery slope. David's need for love, acceptance, approval, and intimacy was something he battled from his childhood. As long as he was staying close to God, he was satisfied. No one in the Bible wrote prayers and psalms to God the way David did. He is iconic for his passionate expressions of love and dependency on God. He knew where to go to get his needs met. He knew God. However, his relationship with God was built from a place of despair and great dependence on God, when all he had was God. God was his everything. As he became more and more successful and surrounded by people that loved and respected him, he started getting his desires fulfilled outside of his time with God. Not to say that becoming successful, or being surrounded with people that love and respect you is a bad thing. It is a gift from God. God wanted that for David. God is the one that chose David to be king. But, David chose to step away from God. God sent Nathan not only to bring vindication to Bathsheba, but in hope that David would wake up.

Then David said to Nathan, "I have sinned against the Lord." Nathan replied, 'The Lord has taken away your sin. You are not going to die. But because by doing this you have shown utter contempt for the Lord, the son born to you will die.'

"After Nathan had gone home, the Lord struck the child that Uriah's wife had borne to David, and he became ill. David pleaded with God for the child. He fasted and spent the nights lying in sackcloth on the ground. The elders of his household stood beside him to get him up from the ground, but he refused, and he would not eat any food with them.

"On the seventh day, the child died. David's attendants were afraid to tell him that the child was dead, for they thought, 'While the child was still living, he wouldn't listen to us when we spoke to him. How can we now tell him the child is dead? He may do something desperate.' David noticed that his attendants were whispering among themselves, and he realized that the child was dead. 'Is the child dead?' he asked. 'Yes,' they replied, 'he is dead.' Then David got up from the ground. After he had washed, put on lotions and changed his clothes, he went into the house of the Lord and worshipped. Then he went to his own house, and at his request they served him food, and he ate. His attendants asked him, 'Why are you acting in this way? While the child was alive, you fasted and wept, but now that the child is dead, you get up and eat!'

"He answered, 'While the child was still alive, I fasted and wept. I thought, "Who knows? The Lord may be gracious to me and let the child live." But now that he is dead, why should I go on fasting? Can I bring him back again? I will go to him, but he will not return to me.'

"Then David comforted his wife Bathsheba, and he went to her and made love to her. She gave birth to a son, and they named him Solomon. The Lord loved him; and because the Lord loved him, he sent word through Nathan the prophet to name him Jedidiah" (2 Samuel 12:7-25 NIV).

It seems David was sincerely distraught over the baby, yet, I also think he was aware of how deeply this was going to hurt Bathsheba's heart, yet again. Now she was going to lose the only thing she had left. I think David had Bathsheba on his heart when he was fasting and pleading with God to spare the child. It shows that after the child died, David went to Bathsheba and comforted her. He cared about her. He cared about what he had done. God knew Bathsheba was going to experience yet another devastating loss. We see again, God already had a plan to redeem her pain. He set that plan in motion almost immediately after her loss.

He sent David to comfort her. Because David was listening to him again. Sin had been atoned for. The wages of sin is death. We now have Jesus to atone for our sins, but David had to pay with a son. God paid once and for all with his son. Jesus.

Now David and Bathsheba were free to begin again. Bathsheba had to walk in forgiveness. She had to choose to either stay in the past, or persevere in to her future. She decided to clothe herself in dignity. She chose to laugh at the days to come, even when it felt like those days were laughing at her. She is our example of how to handle the most difficult times in life. The Bible clearly tells us she mourned when she needed to mourn. It also shows us she allowed her pain to pull her forward instead of allowing it to pin her down.

Even in a palace you can feel like you're in prison. Yet, if we choose to align our mind with truth, God's truth, and what He says about us, we can take that prison and turn it into a palace. A palace is where we belong. We are children of The King. The King of all Kings. He says you are His son, His daughter. You are His princess, His prince, the heir to everything He owns. If that truth begins to sink in, and we decide to believe it, there will be no prison big enough to hold you. You will choose to stay in the palace and let your daddy fight the battle for you.

~ CHAPTER SIX ~

Prisoner of Hope or Circumstance

BATHSHEBA IS A GREAT example of how to never lose sight of who we really are. She was a virtuous woman. She was a woman of noble character. She was a woman who knew her God. She was a woman who was convinced of her true identity. How do I know that? I know that because she never lost her identity. Even when others were trying to put a new title over her real identity.

She could have identified with bitterness. She could have come into agreement with the enemy of her soul telling her she was cursed, and she would never know true joy or contentment again. Like the story in the Bible of Naomi, her husband and two sons died leaving her a desolate widow. She was left with no one except a loyal daughter in law named Ruth. Naomi chose to identify with her circumstances instead of her true identity. She went as far as changing her name to Mara, which means bitter. She told people, "Don't call me Naomi anymore, call me Mara, for the Almighty has made my life very bitter" (Ruth 1:20 NIV).

There are people who choose to come into agreement with the enemy. They focus on the circumstance they are in. We all have the choice to do that. There's a song I chose to play over and over during a difficult time in my life titled, "Even when it hurts," by Hillsong United. One line in the song says, "Even when it hurts like hell, I'll praise you!" That might seem offensive to some. However, if you have tasted the bitterness of losing someone you love to disease, grieving the death of a child, tasted the bitterness of betrayal or gone through the pain of divorce, you know it will hurt like hell to lift up a sacrifice of praise during that season. Once you have tasted pain to the level of wanting to change your name to Mara, that song hits home. It strikes the chord of your very soul. When Mara is staring you in the face, you have to choose whether to identify with the name bitterness or choose to start singing praise to the God that can bring the peace that will pass your finite understanding. We have to choose to say, "Even if it hurts like hell, because God it does, I will praise you. I will choose to be a prisoner of hope, not circumstance. My circumstances will change, but my hope never changes. God is my hope and Jesus is my choice. He promises to make every bitter circumstance bow to His beauty. Therefore, in the presence of His beauty, my mess must become beautiful."

Bathsheba gets word that God has seen her. David is sorry. He has repented. God has vindicated her. He sent the prophet Nathan to vindicate her. If only that was the end of her pain. Unfortunately, the wages of sin is death. Sin comes to collect its payment. Why did it have to be her baby? Why? Why did the baby have to die? Why? Because Jesus hadn't come yet. This is when it hits home. The ultimate sacrifice for all sin was yet to come. Jesus, The Messiah, the ultimate sacrifice.

Bathsheba is mentioned in the lineage of Jesus Christ. She is the great grandmother, the foremother of Jesus the Messiah, who would come and take away the sins of the world. However, she is also the foremother of both Mary the mother of Jesus, and Joseph the earthly father of Jesus. Why is this so amazing? As we continue on this journey through the life of Bathsheba, we learn she has four sons with David. Solomon is the son that Mary the mother of Jesus will come through. Bathsheba's other son Nathan, is who Joseph, the earthly father of Jesus, will come through. David had many wives and many sons. But God chose only one of his wives, Bathsheba. God chose Bathsheba to be the queen mother of the son of David, Solomon, that would succeed him on the throne. The very throne that Jesus himself will come back to reign upon. He chose Bathsheba, to be the foremother of Jesus Christ. Why would God take such incredible notice of this woman? What was it about Bathsheba that she was chosen? I think we are beginning to see the answer to that question unfold. She was a woman of great virtue. A woman to be praised. A noble woman indeed. A woman who could laugh at the days to come. Because Bathsheba was a woman who knew intimately the one who ordered those days. The same God who was caring for Bathsheba as she grieved the death of her one and only son, had already ordered the day ahead that would bring His one and only son, through her, to once and for all take away the sting of death.

Bathsheba was just recovering from the loss of her husband and everything she held dear. She had held on to the one promise of hope, her baby. Now she has just been given word, that promise is dead.

How do you keep going when it seems all hope is dead? This is when it is so important to apply the power of choice and the free will we have been given.

A BEAUTIFUL MESS

I can choose death, or I can choose life. I have a jar holding the pens on my desk that says, "Today, I choose joy!" I look at that many times a day when I'm in my office. Every time I look at it, I am reminded to choose again. I have had different times in my life when I knew I had a choice to make. I was either going to identify with the circumstances going on in my life, or was going to hold on with all I had left to my true identity. My identity as a prisoner of hope.

One of those times came when Kevin and I had been married about two years. We found out I was pregnant. We were so excited! We announced it to our whole family, church, and anyone who would listen. In the midst of the excitement of the baby, my mom was diagnosed with breast cancer. It was devastating. They had found it in her lymph nodes and we were facing a daunting battle for her life. I couldn't imagine having my first baby without my mom there. I was only 23 years old and very close to my mom. During my mom's battle with cancer, I lost the baby to miscarriage. It was such a devastating experience. I was so young, and I had no idea what was going on. The pain in my heart equaled the pain I was experiencing in my body from the miscarriage. It was an ugly experience. We wanted to have a baby so badly. My heart was hurting and afraid. I wondered; how could God let something like this happen? We were serving Him in full time youth ministry. Why would God take away the joy of a baby while my mom is battling for her life?

But I will tell you one thing; I did not let my heart become hard towards God. I began to face things I thought I would never be able to go through. Thankfully my mom did recover, and I became pregnant again with my now 24-year-old baby girl, Kelci Noelle. Her name Kelci means victory, and Noelle means a gift from God. But I was faced again with a battle when newly pregnant, I almost miscarried Kelci. I believe I was miscarrying. But something rose up within me the night I began to bleed and cramp when pregnant with her. I began to pray in a way I never prayed before. I began to quote promises of scripture back to God. Reminding Him of His promises to me through His word. I was not asking for anything out of line with the scriptures. I began to claim the blood of Jesus over my womb. I began to pray against the spirit of death and miscarriage. A warrior was being birthed. Not only the one in my womb, but it was starting with me. God touched my body that night and I knew distinctly I had been touched by God. In the morning as I was making the bed, I began to sing an old chorus I had grown up singing in the church. "He touched me, oh He touched me, and oh the joy that floods my soul, something happened, and now

I know, He touched me, and made me whole." Not only did He touch me, but the day of my baby shower for Kelci, was the first day my mom had all her hair back after losing it from chemotherapy, she didn't have to wear a wig anymore. He had touched her too. He had healed her of breast cancer. We celebrated big that day! However, I had one more victory lap to run before finally seeing my Kelci girl in the flesh.

The last lap began on the day of one of my prenatal check-up visits to my doctor. She had found something she was concerned about. She explained to me that my uterus was heart shaped, and as darling as that might sound, it was not good news. She explained how that would make it impossible for me to ever carry a baby full term. It was impossible for the baby to grow to full size due to the baby being unable to turn and drop into the birth canal. The baby would only grow in a breach position, making it impossible to deliver a baby naturally. I would have to have a scheduled C-Section. I was devastated and scared. She then told me she wanted to send me and Kevin to Stanford University Hospital to be seen by specialists. There they could equip Kevin and I with all the information on how to care for our preemie baby.

We went to Stanford where they examined me and showed Kevin and I what we were going to be dealing with. We went home from Stanford that day loaded down with all kinds of books and materials to study and prepare for our upcoming challenges ahead. My heart was heavy again. However, something deep down inside my soul was not settled. I was not ready to accept this as my truth. I believed God made my body to deliver a baby naturally, and that it was His design for that baby to grow and mature to the time frame He set, not any doctor. I told Kevin, "I'm not going to have a C-Section. And this baby is going to develop and mature on God's timeline. I will deliver this baby girl full term and naturally. He touched me before, and He is going to touch me again." Kevin was in agreement.

We began to pray and believe for the miracle. I asked my doctor at my next visit what the chances were of delivering this baby naturally and at full term. She looked right at me and said, "Valeri Noonan, it would take a miracle." I looked right back at her and said, "Okay, good, because I believe in miracles!" She was one of the very best doctors of the Silicon Valley. She wasn't a Christian and she wasn't real impressed by my faith. However, we had a mutual respect for one another, and we were beginning to build a relationship. She just smiled at me. Well, from that point on I was blessed with an ultrasound every few weeks during the duration of my pregnancy. So, as time was getting closer to my scheduled C-Section, I would ask the ultra sound technician each time I went in, "Is the baby in position yet?" This meaning, the baby had turned and was getting in position for delivery. Each time I asked, I hoped it would be the answer I was praying for. I would usually get a perplexed look from the technician, as if they were confused at my question. I knew they were wondering why I was asking such a question when the whole reason I was there was due to my high risk pregnancy. Some would just say no and keep looking. One answered, "No, the baby is breach, I don't think the baby is supposed to turn."

We were at one of our last ultrasound appointments before my scheduled C-Section. I asked the question as usual. This time we had a sweet technician that didn't talk very much. I asked her the question as she began my ultra sound. She looked at the monitor quietly for a moment as she moved the ultra sound wand over my belly, and then quietly answered, "Yes, it looks like the baby has turned and is starting to drop." I sat up and stared at her and said, "What did you just say?" She then looked back at me like I was crazy. She then said it again, "Yes, the baby has turned." I looked up at Kevin and said, "Did you just hear that?" He looked back and said, "I think so. Did she just say she turned?" "Yes! She turned!" I declared.

I couldn't wait to get to my next OBGYN appointment! Dr. Hall was very thorough. She was a great doctor. She said let's do an ultra sound and make sure everything is how it should be. As she was doing the ultra sound she said with a smile, "Well, I guess we can talk about canceling the scheduled C-Section if that is something you would like to do." I smiled back and said, "Yes, that is what I want to do." I not only delivered Kelci Noelle naturally, but God made sure to show off, she was born over two weeks past her due date. When Kelci was born, she had a white film on her skin. I asked the doctor what that was. She told me the medical terminology for it. Then, she said, "Basically it's what happens when the baby is over-baked." I looked at her and smiled and said, "Well, that's a miracle isn't it?" She let out a little chuckle and replied, "I guess you could call it that." Then she looked at me so sincerely and said, "Congratulations Valeri Noonan, she is beautiful!" I smiled back at her and said, "Thank you, Dr. Hall. For everything! And yes, you're right, she is beautiful, God did an extra great job with this one!" She smiled and quietly said, "Agreed!" It was a new day. I got my miracle! Was it difficult? Of course. Was it worth it all? Of course!

Kelci was the center of our universe! She was so smart, kind, hilarious, and in charge! She had a tiny bit of blonde hair, and the biggest blue eyes we had ever seen. She was such a beautiful baby girl. She was like a bright ray of sunshine to Kevin and me, and anyone she came in contact with. People would constantly stop me in stores to tell me what piercingly beautiful eyes she had. And believe me when those eyes were looking at you, you knew you were being looked at. We call her our sunshine girl to this day, anywhere Kelci goes she brings sunshine. She also brings Son-shine to the kingdom of darkness, and for that I know why I battled and didn't give up! Sometimes you just can't give up! There is too much at stake! I believe Bathsheba felt that same warrior spirit over her circumstances. She was chosen, and something in her knew she needed to keep fighting.

Bathsheba became pregnant again and she gave birth to another son. It was custom in that day for the father to name the first son. David named their son Solomon. Solomon is a Hebrew baby name. In Hebrew the meaning of the name Solomon is Peace. Finally some peace had come to this couple. Bathsheba had her precious baby boy. "Then David comforted Bathsheba, his wife, and slept with her. She became pregnant and gave birth to a son, and David named him Solomon. The LORD loved the child, and because the LORD loved him, he sent word through Nathan the prophet to name him Jedidiah" (2 Samuel 24-25 NLT, NIV).

This is the only mention of the name Jedidiah in all the Bible. The meaning of the name Jedidiah is, beloved of God which can also be said; belonging to God. The meaning of the name Lemuel: to God; dedicated to God; belonging to God. The three names of Solomon combined. Peaceful, loved by, and belonging to God. Solomon was all those things. He brought peace to David and Bathsheba. He was a constant reminder to them of God's love for them, and that they still belonged to Him. God wants to remind us of that same message. He is the author of peace. He wants to bring peace into our mess, by reminding us that He loves us and that we still belong to Him. Peace comes to any circumstance by knowing we are loved by God and that nothing will ever be able to snatch us out of His love because we belong to God.

David needed to hear from God. He needed to hear Nathan say, "Call him Jedidiah." We don't see where David changed Solomon's name to Jedidiah, or that Solomon was referred to as Jedidiah. We know him as Solomon. So why wouldn't David obey God after all he had been through? Nathan wasn't instructing David to change Solomon's name. Jedidiah was what God said about Solomon. It was God telling David he was forgiven. This son was blessed. David was still God's beloved. Interestingly the name David means, beloved. God was telling His beloved son to call his son, beloved. Beloved of God. This son belonged to God. He was giving His approval over Solomon. God was also loving David back to His heart. There was redemption even in a mess that David had created. God brought unmerited grace through Solomon.

Here we see God sending Nathan to David and Bathsheba once again to deliver His word over the new circumstance. Aren't you starting to see God in a new way? This is not a mean, judgmental God of the Old Testament. This is a loving father. A very in tune, very involved father. I love this picture of God. How had I missed this version, throughout the years of reading this account in the Bible? How is it before He seemed more like a scary, punishing father? Yet now, reading the exact same scriptures, I see Him so differently. He is so much better. It's the same in our lives and in our circumstances. It is like when two people can go through the same challenge and come out with completely different versions. One might find hope, another Mara. It's when the truth becomes more alive *in* our circumstances that we can see things more clearly.

Psalm 51 shows us David, the man after God's heart is back. The entire Psalm is an apology of David to God in response to his sin with Bathsheba:

"Be gracious to me, O God, according to Your

loving kindness; According to the greatness of Your compassion blot out my transgressions. Wash me thoroughly from my iniquity, and cleanse me from my sin. For I know my transgressions, and my sin is ever before me. Against You, You only, I have sinned and done what is evil in Your sight, So that You are justified when You speak And blameless when You judge. Behold, I was brought forth in iniquity, And in sin my mother conceived me. Behold, You desire truth in the innermost being, And in the hidden part You will make me know wisdom. Purify me with hyssop, and I shall be clean; Wash me, and I shall be whiter than snow. Make me to hear joy and gladness, Let the bones which You have broken rejoice. Hide Your face from my sins, and blot out all my iniquities. Create in me a clean heart, O God, and renew a steadfast spirit within me. Do not cast me away from Your presence, and do not take Your Holy Spirit from me. Restore to me the joy of Your salvation, and sustain me with a willing spirit. *Then* I will teach transgressors Your ways, and sinners will be converted to You" (Psalm 51:1-13 NAS).

David is a great example for us to follow, even in his sin and restoration. Many people think if they do something terrible in life that it makes them unworthy to ever be loved by God. It isn't true. The key point that David teaches us through this passage is that when we do choose the wrong path, we must recognize it and then move closer to God instead of being like Adam and Eve trying to hide from God. Instead of being angry at God, or blaming someone else, we accept responsibility and ask God to forgive us.

David was all the good things written about him. He was kind, he was strong, he was talented, he was brave, he was godly, and he loved God passionately. He was loyal, he was faithful, he was humble, he was fair, and he was thankful! He loved God and he sought after God. He included God in his life.

But David was also human, and made some very bad choices. All humans will have moments in their lives that both honor and dishonor God. But the dishonor will not destroy us permanently. Our choices are not what will keep us away from God, it is our response to the correction God brings. Are you willing to listen, and to humble your heart, and receive the fact that you don't have the ability to do it in your own strength? God sees the places where the enemy tried to break your heart. He knows about the pain of your past, your childhood, or your current situation. He only wants to heal those places. He only desires to fill those voids with love. His love that satisfies, and never leaves you hungry.

My husband and I often get comments on how great our marriage is. We've been married 28 years now and we always respond to people saying, "Yes, we do have a great marriage. However, we could blow this thing up any time, any day, if we didn't stay submitted to God, and committed to one another." Not that we would ever want or desire to blow things up, but the truth is that we are human and we will not have a good marriage if we stop listening to God and each other. Anything good in our lives is from God. We must never forget that truth. We also need to remember that anything messy in our lives can be made beautiful when God is at the center.

How about you? Do you have a circumstance that you've been prisoner to? Do you want to walk out of that prison and begin again? Why not become a prisoner of hope instead of circumstance? I can attest to this, when you reframe your life in this way, you can make it through anything and come out better instead of bitter. It is as simple as deciding today. Today is your new beginning. We see David and Bathsheba at the place of new beginnings. They have heard from God. They have been vindicated by God. David is now caring for Bathsheba's heart. Moving forward, they will have to walk out forgiveness. David will have to choose to identify with his forgiveness from God, and Bathsheba, and not continue to wear the blanket of shame the enemy will want to keep him in. Bathsheba will have to walk in forgiveness daily. The enemy will want to remind her of all the reasons she has to resent David. The memories will come back. She will have to choose to renew her mind with forgiveness for David. She will have to remember to continually keep her eyes on God, remembering what God did for her, instead of what David did to her. In addition, she must remember, if God can forgive David, she can also forgive him. There is beauty being offered in spite of the mess. They have their new baby boy, Solomon. He is blessed and favored by God. He is their constant reminder of the new beginning offered to them by God.

CHAPTER SEVEN

Begin Again

BATHSHEBA HAS HER NEW baby boy, Solomon. She has the blessing of God over her boy. She has been vindicated by God. David has repented and his heart is tender towards her. She is beginning to get back up and dream a new dream. She has a boy to raise. She knows God is with her. He rescued her when no one else could. She must have felt strength from knowing God saw her. Not only did He see her, but He came and rescued her. We will see as we continue, just how God left a tangible piece of Himself in the palace to look after her. Nathan the prophet never completely fades into the background again. He is a friend not only to David but also now to David's precious wife, Bathsheba.

Nathan is a foreshadowing of the Holy Spirit. He was always there. He was there to convict, to comfort, and to assist. As I write this I can't help but feel an overwhelming sense of gratefulness in my heart for the Holy Spirit. I am so thankful we can simply ask for help, no matter where we are, what is going on; the Holy Spirit is right there with me. I don't need a person to show up. The person, the Holy Spirit of God, is right here in me and with me. We have so much to be thankful for as we look at this story from the other side of the cross. What a gift. We can be forgiven of any sin in an instant. All we have to do is believe that Jesus is who He says He is, that He is the Son of God Who came to take away the sins of the world. We can simply ask Him to forgive our sins and wash us clean. Then we only have to accept the free gift of His love and forgiveness and a brand new start! Wow! I think the wonder of God's love is oftentimes more than we are able to comprehend. Religion asks something of us, requires we do the work in some way. Religion says, "Do." Jesus says, "Done! I did it all for you. Now just take my hand and let me show you a life, unlimited." The limitless life in Jesus is incredible.

Bathsheba has a new road ahead now. She is choosing to walk in forgiveness, with her head held high. She has to choose to clothe herself in dignity, trust God, and not be shaken by distractions. Where did she find the strength to do this? She relied on

God's strength instead of striving in her own strength. I want to learn from Bathsheba how to be a woman that is not striving. She was clothed in strength and dignity. I want to remember to clothe myself in God's strength daily. She allowed God to care for her. She seems like a woman who knew how loved she was by God.

It is the same for you and me. In order to live out our God-designed purpose in life, we have to be convinced that we are loved by God. We must be convinced He is with us, and will always come through when we need Him. However, the only way we can be convinced of this truth is through the challenging times in life. The times we want to blame Him. The times we might think we can't handle the pressure anymore. Those are the times He will show Himself more powerful than we could ever imagine. The key is what we choose. We must choose to allow Him in and choose to let Him love us. If we do, just like Bathsheba, we will have the ability to laugh at the days to come.

Kelci was about two years old and we were loving life with our baby girl. Yet, we were feeling ready to have another baby. We thought it would be good to have our kids two to three years apart. The first year of trying for another baby came and went. Kelci turned three, and she started saying, with her heavy lisp, "Mommy, I really want a baby thithter, when is God going to bring her?" I'd usually just respond with, "I know baby! Keep praying." One day, however, it wasn't that easy. We were driving home from shopping and all of a sudden she pulled her binky out of her mouth with her big blue eyes sternly staring at me in the rearview mirror. Very passionately, she said, "Mom, why isn't God bringing us a baby? I really want a baby thithter! Everybody else has one!" It's weird how kids can sometimes just cut right to the point. I felt the same way. Why God? Why is this such a difficult process? Pregnancy test after pregnancy test. Let down after let down. It did feel like everyone else had a baby. It hurt so bad when she said it. I looked in the rearview mirror at my little miracle in the back seat nestled in her car seat, looking back at me. With tears streaming down my face, hidden behind my sunglasses, I said, "I know Kelc, I want one too! Really bad!"

A few months later I found out I was pregnant! It was so exciting! The timing couldn't have been better. At least that's what I thought. My dad had just been diagnosed with an inoperable brain tumor. My life was rocked to the core. We were in the middle of processing and dealing with the news of his condition. So finding out I was pregnant felt like a kiss from heaven. It also felt so good to know my dad would at least know about the baby. Even if he wouldn't live to see him or her. My dad was given a maximum of six months to live after his diagnosis. He lasted four months. It was Christmas of 1997 when my dad starting showing signs that something was not right with him. He was a very articulate man. He had a vocabulary that was admirable. He was brilliant and very quick witted. So, when he started being unable to finish a simple sentence, we knew something was off. At first, my mom thought it was just from the stress of the Christmas season - things amped up so much at the church during the holidays. The church put on a second to none Christmas presentation. It was the Christmas event of the community. My dad did everything with excellence. It was January of 1998 when my dad was diagnosed with a glioblastoma. The worst kind of brain tumor you can have. He went from being the strongest person I knew to a man fighting for his life. It was so fast. He was only sixty one years old. He was in great shape. He had a thriving church in one of the most difficult areas in the world to pastor, the city of Richmond, California. He grew that church from about thirty retired people to close to a thousand people of all ages and ethnic backgrounds. My dad loved being a pastor, and it showed in the success that he was made to be one. It was the most amazing church to grow up in.

A BEAUTIFUL MESS

It was a multi-cultural, multi-generational church. It had people from all walks of life come through the doors; yet once they were inside, everyone was family. I loved that church. Everyone in the church - white, black, Asian, rich, poor, homeless, and successful - loved him dearly and knew they were loved by him as well. He died four months after his diagnosis. It was a difficult time for our family and the church.

The day before he died I was at my parent's house. He noticed I was upset even though he was struggling with his mental processing. He looked at me from across the room, he was dialed in. He spoke the words I'd heard him say thousands of times growing up, "Everything okay, honey?" I could barely gather myself to answer him. I was sitting in his recliner chair in the family room with my feet elevated, and my heart rapidly sinking. I had started showing all the signs of miscarriage again. I was devastated. I didn't want to say anything to him, but it was taking everything in me to keep it together. As I answered I started to cry, "I think I might be losing this baby!" I'll never forget how he came over to that chair. For a few minutes, he was my strong dad again. He then spoke the comforting words to me I had heard him say thousands of times before, "Everything is going to be alright honey bunch." He began praying for me. I didn't realize it would be the last time he ever prayed over me. He struggled to get my name out, but he prayed a faith-filled prayer like he always prayed. Kevin came to the house to get me. We had to get to a doctor's appointment about forty-five minutes away, on the other side of the San Francisco Bay. Before we left, I hugged my mom and then, I hugged my dad. It was the last time I ever hugged him. It was the last time I ever saw my dad again.

My doctor confirmed I was miscarrying and told me to go home and get some rest. The next day, the doctor called. After telling her my symptoms, she confirmed I had miscarried the baby. We set up a follow-up appointment and then I hung up. I couldn't believe it. I started to get in the shower when the phone rang again. This time it was my mom on the other end. She said, "Valeri, is Kevin home?" I said, "No, why? Is something wrong with daddy?" She asked if I knew when Kevin would be there. I said, "Just tell me! Is he okay?" She said, "I would just feel better if Kevin was with you right now." I didn't know then that she had called Kevin and told him – he was on his way home from the office. I blurted out, "Did he die? Mother, is daddy gone?" She answered quietly, "Yes baby, he's gone." At that moment I felt my entire body go numb. I felt my ears closing up like I was going deaf. I felt pain so deep inside my soul it was unbearable! She said, "Valeri, are you okay?" I said, "Yes, are you okay Mama?" She was the strongest woman I'd ever known, or will ever know. She answered with such strength in her voice, "Yes, I'm okay. Your daddy is in heaven with Jesus. He was on his way out of his office at the church and going down the hall to put some things in storage when he dropped to the ground." The paramedic told my mom he was gone before he even hit the floor. He literally was walking out of his office that represented his ministry and service for Jesus on this earth, and walked right into heaven. Jesus was there to greet him. Wow! My dad refused to stop. He hadn't been doing very well the day he died. My mom told me that she had tried to talk him into staying home that day, but he refused. He told her he needed to be at the church. So she drove him there. He was staying busy by cleaning out his office. He was packing up because he knew his work on earth was coming to a close. He was relocating. And when she got home, it wasn't long before she received the call he was gone. I told her I would get ready and head over.

When I hung up the phone, I could hardly breathe. I decided to get in the shower so I could get ready to go to my parent's house. I was trying to process physically, emotionally, mentally, and spiritually the loss of my baby, and my dad. Why would God take them both? And why would He take them at the same time? As I stood in the shower, I was overcome with grief. It hurt to the core of my being. I dropped to the floor of the shower and began dry heaving. It was like my body was trying to purge itself of the pain. It took a while for the tears to come. But then they came. I sat there, on the floor of the shower, sobbing with the water running over me. While the water ran over me and down the drain, all my hope and strength went down that drain with it. I didn't think I was going to be able to make it through this one.

Kevin arrived home and found me in a heap in the shower. My life had just changed forever. It was a new day. It was my initiation into loss, grief, disappointment, and pain like I had never dealt with before. I was faced with a decision - would this make me a better person? Or would this make me a bitter person? It was a process. I had to go through all the stages of loss and grief. But what I came out of it with, was, with God, I could handle much more than I dreamt I was capable of. The scripture David penned in Psalm 23 hit home for me in a whole new way. I never fully understood it until this point in my life. He writes, "Even though I walk through the valley of the shadow of death, I will fear no evil, for your rod and staff they comfort me." I felt the comfort that only Jesus could bring me during those days. But I had to allow that comfort. I had to welcome

His comfort, instead of blaming Him for the pain. I wouldn't trade anything I've gone through in this life of mine if it meant I had to give back those precious times with Jesus. He really is the peace that passes our understanding. The key is to keep walking. Don't sit down in the valley of the shadow of death. Keep holding the hand of Jesus. He will lead you through that valley, and out of the valley. It is only temporary. The reason David calls it the valley of the shadow of death is because Jesus is the light in the valley. You can't have shadows in complete darkness. Keeping our eyes on Jesus during the dark times in life will keep the darkness from taking over.

Again we're reminded of Bathsheba and how she was able to handle the most cruel circumstances with dignity. The woman who learned how to handle the days in life that seemed to be laughing in her face. She kept her dignity and remained in strength. Don't you feel like that sometimes? You feel like your circumstances are laughing in your face? What do you do? I can tell you what I did. I think Bathsheba did this as well. I chose what side I was going to camp on. I chose to begin again and to not give up. Believe me I had to make the choice. I remember wanting to give up. I wanted to be mad at God. During the time all of this was going on I felt like God asked me a question. I was angry because God took my dad at such a young age and it didn't seem fair, especially since he had devoted his life to ministry. I remember saying to Kevin, "I want out of this ministry gig if this is what we get to look forward to! We will give our lives to ministry only to have God take us out with some terrible disease and leave our kids without parents. I can't do this. I don't want to do this."

I was speaking out of pain and fear. Kevin was struggling with it as well. My dad was his mentor in ministry and one of his best friends. We needed my dad. Then God asked me the question I'll never forget. I felt Him speak so clearly, "Valeri, am I still God? Am I still God when everything around you doesn't make any sense. Or am I only God when everything is going how you think it should be going?" Being a Christian my entire life you think that would have been an easy question to answer. However, it stopped me in my tracks. You see, I knew God was still God. But if He was God in any circumstance, it meant He was still good in every circumstance. It was always easy for me to declare that God was good all the time, until this time. I finally said with a lot of tears, "Yes, you are still God. Even when everything is falling apart around me, and I don't understand any of it. I believe you are still God, and I believe somehow you are still good."

He is still God. And God is always good. Even

when everything around you might scream the opposite. Something shifts inside of you when you declare that before you see anything change around you. It helped me. I can't totally explain how, but I can just tell you this. When you choose to trust God when it doesn't make any sense, He becomes closer than you've ever known. He will comfort you in ways that won't make any sense to your natural mind. It really is a choice. Are you going to camp on the side of being a victim? A prisoner of circumstance? Or are you going to choose hope? Will you choose to be a prisoner of hope? You can tell yourself and your circumstances how it is going to go. It is learning to align your mind with truth even when it doesn't feel true. God promises to turn everything around for the good of those who trust Him. However, when you find yourself standing over the open grave of all your dreams, and you have no control over any of it, it will take grit. It will take perseverance. It will take wanting to be better over choosing to be bitter. It might sound cliché, but I think that's the whole point. Sometimes we are waiting for a revelation, when the obvious is staring us right in the face. We want to be rescued, because a rescue requires no work on our end. If we are going to get to another level, it requires a climb. I'd rather go higher, wouldn't you? That is the point of difficulties. To make you stronger. To release you of being dependent upon anything or anyone for your security or joy, besides God.

Through the difficult times I received something I would have never found without going through the pain. I found out what I am made of. I had to dig to the deepest part of me to see if there was enough to survive with. What I found was that I can go through much more than I ever believed possible. I was twenty eight years old when I discovered the incredible power of God sustaining me, holding me, loving me, giving me strength I never thought possible. He also showed me something else that only pain can reveal. Nothing can break me unless I let it break me. I could've fallen apart. I could've given up. I could've gotten into agreement with despair. Instead, I decided to dig. Like a palm tree, I was dry and very thirsty. I felt like I had been blown over by the strong winds called the hurricane of life. I felt like I was bent down to the ground under the weight of grief and hopelessness. Yet, something in me managed to start digging. Like the roots of the palm tree - they keep pushing down, down, down, until they hit water. I began to dig down, down, down, crying out to God like I had never cried out before. I began receiving scriptures and memorizing them, quoting them back to God and reminding Him of His word. Little did I know, just like the palm tree, I was growing. It wasn't evident yet from above the ground of my heart, just as the tree is bent over above the ground in a storm. But my roots were growing. They were getting deeper and deeper. Soon I would pop back up just like the Palm tree does once the storm passes.

It was time to begin again. I allowed myself to go through the normal grieving process. Grieving is a gift from God. It is the key to getting *through* the valley of the shadow of death. David penned it so well when he wrote the 23rd Psalm, "Though I walk *through* the valley of the shadow of death I will fear no evil, for you will guide and comfort me." Grief is different from depression. Grief has an expiration to it. Depression can last a lifetime. It is the most important thing you can do when you face loss of any kind. Allow yourself to grieve. Remind yourself it is a gift from God. The stages of grief are all okay. They are normal. They help you come out on the other side of tragedy, healed and victorious. You must keep walking through the valley of the shadow of death, and not sit down in it. There has to be light in order for there to be shadows. The enemy wants us to focus on the shadow of death in our circumstance. However, Jesus is the light that will dispel those shadows. We must focus on what allows those shadows to even exist. It's the light. Jesus isn't a shadow. He is the light.

As I began to feel stronger I really wanted to try for

another baby. Kelci was still adamant about having that baby sister. She was still praying faithfully for God to bring her a sister. I believe the prayers of children are some of the most powerful prayers in the universe. In Mark 10:15 Jesus says, "I tell you the truth, anyone who doesn't receive the Kingdom of God like a child will never enter it." Kelci didn't pray as though there was an option of God saying no. She prayed like there was no option except yes. What if we prayed that way? Children are relentless. At least mine are. If there is something they really want, they don't just ask me once. They don't just ask me twice. They actually don't stop talking about it until they get my response. They want to tell me all the reasons they think I should get whatever it is they want for them. Even when I don't understand why they want whatever it is they are asking for, it gets my attention because I know how badly they want it. The truth is, I always want to give my kids what they want. There is nothing better than seeing my children happy. God feels the same way about us. Of course there are times I can't always give my kids what they are asking for; but whenever I can, I do. Unless I know what they are asking for won't be good for them. Those are the times I try to instruct them. Try to lead them in the direction of something else that would be much better for them. All in all, that is God. I wonder how many times we miss getting the things we desire so deeply because we don't believe God wants to give us good things. Maybe we give up too soon? I have learned that no matter what we ask, God will answer. It might not be the answer we want at the time, but He will answer. It might not make sense at all. It might even seem like He is being mean. However, we can't give up during those times. We must always begin again. Kelci was ready to believe and persistently ask God for that sister. So we did not give up. Instead, we began again.

We started what felt like the merry-go-round of wondering if I was pregnant each month. That is a very difficult time to be in. If you are going through that right now as you're reading this, don't give up! God knows what He is doing. Keep believing. Nothing worthwhile is easy. It is hard, but it will always be worth it.

I took yet another home pregnancy test, and though the lines were faint, it read positive. I was so excited! Kevin and I didn't want to tell anyone for a while, just to be on the safe side. Once I went to my doctor it was confirmed that I was indeed pregnant. It was at my first ultra sound appointment that Dr. Hall was trying to locate the baby's heartbeat. At first, it wasn't a big deal, but the longer she was searching, my heart was starting to sink. She looked at me with that all too familiar look and said, "Valeri, I can't locate a heartbeat, there isn't one." I couldn't believe my ears. I just looked at her and said, "What do you mean? The pregnancy test was positive, it said I was pregnant. You said I was pregnant!" She said, "I know Valeri, but the problem is, there isn't a baby." Long story short, I had tested positive for being pregnant. However, something was wrong. The baby never developed so Kevin and I had to make the very difficult decision that I would get a DNC procedure. I wasn't miscarrying this time, so they had to take it out surgically. Once the DNC was over I went to my follow up appointment with Dr. Hall. She yet again had that look on her face. Holding her clip board, she began, "Valeri Noonan, I don't have very good news for you." I said, "What in the world could you tell me now, I just had the pregnancy removed?" She went on to describe to me a very rare complication that happens at conception and requires early treatment. It is called a molar pregnancy. The formal medical term is a hydatidiform mole. Somehow, instead of a baby growing in your womb at conception, the tissue mass can develop into a malignant trophoblastic cancer. I stared at her. I said nothing. She looked at me and said, "Don't worry, it's not like a brain tumor. You can have your uterus removed if you have to." Well, that was great news! She told me she was pretty confident they got everything out when I had my procedure. But if not, we would know because my blood counts would show if there was cancer. I would have to come in every week for blood work. If my blood counts didn't go down, I would have to do chemotherapy. It was a pill form. If the counts returned to normal I would be okay. It literally felt like she hit me in the face with a two-by-four. So, we began the weekly visits to have my blood work done. Every week felt like a month, waiting to hear the results of my blood count.

I am happy to report I did not have to do chemotherapy. Everything went back to normal and we could try again in about six months. I was at a point where I needed to hear from God. I needed to know He was with me. The Bible became a life line for me. I would pray and ask God to please give me a word from Him that I could hold on to. He did. I needed to see the promises of God before my eyes every day. I quoted them. I didn't talk to a lot of people about it, I wanted to keep only positive thoughts and reports in my mind. I knew I needed to stay in tune with faith. I didn't want to hear anything else. I wouldn't listen to people that tried to talk me out of believing God for another baby. You'd think I would have given up. I can only tell you this, I wanted another baby so badly, and I couldn't find anywhere in the scriptures that said I shouldn't believe God for just that. So, I believed.

Kevin and I prayed and believed God would bring us another baby. Of course, Kelci was still fervently praying and believing.

I asked God for a promise. I asked Him to give me a scripture I could hold on to. He gave me John 16:20-24. It was one of those moments when you open your Bible right to a scripture that jumps off the page and into your heart. I opened my Bible and my eyes went right to these verses, "You will grieve, but your grief will suddenly turn to wonderful joy. It will be like a woman suffering the pains of labor. When her child is born, her anguish gives way to joy because she has brought a new baby into the world. So you have sorrow now, but I will see you again; then you will rejoice, and no one can rob you of that joy. At that time you won't need to ask me for anything. I tell you the truth, you will ask the Father directly and he will grant your request because you use my name. Ask using my name, and you will receive, and you will have abundant joy!" In that moment, I knew God had heard my cry. He gave me a promise. I held on to that promise with everything in me.

Months were passing and I was getting discouraged again. It was a Sunday afternoon and Kevin and I were driving home from church. Kevin said, "Val, I felt God speak to me today." I looked at him and said, "Really, what did He say?" He said, "Our baby is on the way." I just sat there for a minute and then, with a lump in my throat, I said, "Oh wow, Kevin, I hope so!" I knew it was significant for Kevin to say that, he wasn't one to say God spoke to him unless he really knew he heard God. He told me God prompted him to kneel down at the altar during the end of the service when he normally would go around praying for other people. He said, "The minute I knelt down I felt God speak to me." He said, "I think God was giving another message to me as well. There are times we all need to humble ourselves before Him, kneel down before Him - not always be the one that has it all together, even if I am the pastor. Sometimes people need to see even that the pastor needs to kneel before God and pray it out." Wow! I knew God was moving. I began to allow myself to get excited. I didn't realize it, but at the time that Kevin was telling me this, I was already pregnant. This time it stuck! I was pregnant with a baby girl! Kelci was elated! So were Kevin and I. There was only one day I had a moment of fear shoot through me like a lightning bolt. I had a terrible cramp in my stomach. It was strong and it hurt so bad I had to sit down. My first reaction was, "Oh no! Please God! I can't lose this baby." Then I remembered the scripture God had given me. The part that said, "No one can rob you of your joy!" You see, once we found out we were having another girl, we named her, Kassidi Joy. I knew God had given me the scripture about giving me back my joy. Kassidi was our joy! God promised me, "No one can rob you of your joy!" I took Him at His word. I obligated God, as my mom taught me to do. I said, "God, thank you for my Kassidi Joy, thank you that nothing can take her away!" As I quoted those verses over and over, my fear left and so did the pain. I never had another problem again.

That December, we got the greatest gift we could ever receive. December 5, Kassidi Joy was born. I'll never forget the words that came out of Dr. Hall's mouth the moment Kassidi was born. She placed Kassidi Joy in my arms, and as I was crying tears of joy, she looked at me with tears in her eyes and said, "You did it Valeri Noonan, you did it!" I looked back at Dr. Hall, full of thankfulness in my heart for her, and said, "No Dr. Hall, God did it, He did it!" She smiled and said the familiar line, "She's beautiful!" I looked down at one of the most beautiful babies I had ever laid my eyes on and said, "Yes, Dr. Hall, she is, isn't she?! God did an exceptional job once again!"

Oh my, did my Kassidi Joy live up to her name. She was the sweetest, easiest baby in the world. She filled our home with such joy! I loved to stare at her, she was perfect in every way. I think this is how God looks at us. He just stares at our perfection and smiles over us. We are His masterpiece. Having children helped me better understand the unconditional love of God. In the book of Zephaniah in the Bible it talks about how God delights over us with gladness, and wants to calm all our fear with His love as He rejoices over us with singing (Zephaniah 3:17 NIV). I felt that kind of love for my babies. As I stared at Kassidi I was in awe of her perfect little dusting of dark brown hair, yummy dark olive skin and dreamy hazel brown eyes. I thought to myself, how did I get so lucky? How did I get the two most gorgeous babies on the planet? I remember staring at Kelci the same way thinking there couldn't be a more perfect human. I was so amazed at how her smooth fair skin highlighted her little dusting of blonde hair and vibrant blue eyes. How could two babies be so opposite and yet equally perfect? I guess the truth is it really didn't matter what they looked like, all I saw was beautiful, because they were mine. It really is like the love of God. When God looks at us all He sees is perfection. He looks at us through the eyes of His unconditional love. Just like Kelci, anywhere I went with my Kassidi, people would stop me and stare at her and say, "She is so beautiful!" I wanted to say, "I know, right?!" But it was more polite to just say, "Thank you." In my heart I felt God delighting over me as I delighted over my baby girl. I would often whisper to God with a smile,

"Thank you so much, you really out did yourself with these babies, they are perfect!" I still whisper that sometimes even now that they are grown. They are still my constant reminder of God's incredible love.

Kelci was five and a half years old when she got her baby sister. She was beside herself with Joy! She loved that baby girl so much that she would grit her teeth so hard when she was holding her she would almost chip her teeth! She would practically shake when she'd look at me and say, "Ooh mom, I love her so much!" (I'm laughing now as I write this, thinking about it. Let's just say, passionate people run in our family!) Kelci also said something else I'll never forget, "See mom.. (insert the heavy lisp, which made it all the better!) I told you God was going to give me a baby sister!"

CHAPTER EIGHT

Guard Your Heart

DAVID AND BATHSHEBA HAD one thing in common. One very important thing they shared. They both knew their God. They both knew God was faithful. They both learned to rely on God as their source. David learned in the sheep pen, all alone, as an outcast to his family. It seems Bathsheba had a wealth of wisdom passed down from her grandfather, father, and most likely, very godly women. She also learned to apply that faith when everything she was taught growing up was being tested. I've found comfort in knowing David and Bathsheba were not perfect. David messed up really bad. However, the one great choice he made was to receive the rebuke of God, repent of his sin, and begin again. His son, as we will see, becomes known as the wisest man who ever lived. God took what good choices David did make in his life along with Bathsheba, and made something beautiful out of their mess.

In the book of Proverbs we see many chapters that start by saying "My son, my son, listen to my instruction." The majority of the Proverbs are Solomon's writings about what his mother and father taught him. His mother was his main tutor. She taught him. She also enlisted another wise tutor to come alongside and teach the young boy. Nathan the prophet was one of Solomon's teachers. This also helps us see again that Nathan was an advocate of Bathsheba. There is no way she would want a man who condemned her as an adulterous woman to have such an influence on her son. Bathsheba loved Nathan. Nathan loved Bathsheba. Nathan was a trusted friend to both Bathsheba and David.

When Bathsheba had her second living son, she was allowed to name the baby. In their culture, the father was to name the firstborn son, and the mother was allowed to name the second. Bathsheba chose to name her son, Nathan. Wow! I wish I could have been there to see that beautiful moment. David looking at Bathsheba and saying, "What would you like to name our son, Bathsheba?" Bathsheba, looking down at the precious little baby boy, this baby representing yet another tangible kiss of redemption from heaven to her heart. Looking through eyes filled with tears of joy at the precious baby in her arms, she whispers, "Nathan." She stares at him, and then again, a bit louder she says, "Nathan, I want to call him Nathan." I wonder if David began to cry. I can only imagine the presence of God that must have been in that room. Nathan. What a mighty man of God he was. He was someone they could trust. He was probably one of the only people who would ever get by with rebuking the king. Nathan, what a beautiful name. I hope Nathan was there to witness that moment. However it played out, I can imagine there were tears of joy. Those are the moments we live for. Those pure, sweet, moments when heaven invades this dark world for a few minutes, and we feel the thick goodness of God's love. What a beautiful mess. There were three people who had been through a lot together up to this point, David, Bathsheba, and Nathan. They are a good picture of how things can turn around, if we just keep our hearts tender towards God, and one another. We all need to keep people in our lives that have the blessing and the credibility to bring rebuke. We need people who will speak into our lives when we need to wake up.

We need help raising our children. Bathsheba was wise. I believe Bathsheba could be called, "The wisest woman who ever lived." How else could she raise such a wise son? Most of the Proverbs, I would assume (not challenging anyone who doesn't believe the way I do), come from what she taught her son. For Solomon to write what he did in Proverbs 31, he had to have seen it modeled. He was basing what he knew of the "Perfect wife and mother" off of what he had observed of his mom. At the beginning of the chapter, he is quoting her directly. Not only is he quoting her words directly, but some versions say it this way, "An oracle his mother taught him." The word oracle means it was prophetic, as if it was coming from the Lord Himself. Sound familiar? Remember, that is what was said about her grandfather, Ahithophel. David and everyone in Israel considered what her grandfather spoke to be so wise, it was as if God Himself was saying it. She was teaching him as if he was already the king. David had many other sons that were older and met the qualifications to succeed him on the throne. Although in the end, we will see that David had made a promise to Bathsheba about Solomon succeeding him as king. She was teaching her young son the ways to live if he were to be a wise king. He was young, but she was raising a king, whether or not he ever sat on a throne.

I think anyone with a son should learn to raise him in this way. They may never actually become a king who rules on a throne. However, we need more kings in this world. Young men who are taught to act like a king. A wise king. A man who can steward their masculinity with honor and dignity. Men who honor themselves by honoring women. Men who live a life that brings honor to The King. As parents, we need to speak oracles over our children. They are the future kings and queens of our world. Bathsheba didn't wait until she had to teach her son the ways of being a godly king, she taught him because she wanted him to be honorable regardless of what title he had over his name. She taught him by example, the value of knowing your identity and the value of keeping the title over your name that you know is true. She may have had many titles put over her name. The title of adulterous woman. The woman who caused the great beloved King David to fall into sin. But she knew what her true identity was. She knew the title over her name was the one God called her by. He called her precious, loved, and virtuous. He vindicated her, when no one else could, or would. She knew she was called to raise her sons to love The King. I think David spoke into Solomon's life as well, from experience. Yet, I think David needed to speak into his son's life more than he did. We will see this later when we look at what happened to David's kids.

Sometimes, if we're not careful, we will forget our true identity. We become weary in trying to remember. I think David knew he was forgiven, but he didn't ever fully let himself off the hook. I think David felt like he needed to be perfect in order to please God fully. He was so good at repenting and accepting God's love and forgiveness. Yet, I see in the latter years of David's life, a man who couldn't fully let himself off the hook for what he did. The enemy knows if we can't fully forgive ourselves, he can keep us in a prison of hiding. Unfortunately his children paid the price. His children needed his strength. David needed to completely own what he did and use it to teach his children how dangerous it is to entertain the temptations of lust, greed, and pride. Instead he said nothing. Much like the family David grew up in, they were well respected and loved God, but they kept secrets regarding their past. The secret of how David was conceived created a much greater problem than if David would have just known the truth. Children will automatically blame themselves when there is a question mark left unanswered. They will also look to fill the void in their heart that only the security of the truth can fill. There is nothing healthy about a secret. Secrets do not cover problems. Secrets just create bigger problems.

David was never fully free after the sin with Bathsheba. From that point on in his life we see a more quiet and passive David. Never before was David passive about anything, especially sin and injustice. However, the enemy knew if he could get David to come into agreement with him regarding his past, he could hold David in the prison of shame regardless of whether or not the door was unlocked.

It was two years after Kassidi Joy was born, and yes, I'm crazy enough to say it, I wanted another baby! I remember telling Kevin, "I just feel like there is one more person out there. When I picture our kids coming back home at Christmas, bringing their families, I just see more than our two girls. There's one more." Kevin said, "There's one more?" I said, "Yes, I want one more, don't you? It feels too perfect. Two beautiful girls. Everything was just too perfect." I know that sounds really weird. It probably is. Yet, I wanted that beautiful mess of more than two kids. My husband is so cool, he always seems to get my weird analogies. He gets the way my brain thinks. That alone shows me that God has one perfect person out there for you. It took my perfect man to be able to understand how this brain works. With an all too familiar grin on his face, he replied, "Well, I guess I could help you out if you really want me to." I replied with a coy, "Well, thank you, I'd like that!" Okay, I'll stop there. He was in favor of trying for another baby. What a stud. My husband is stronger than any man I've ever known, or will ever know. He never runs away from a challenge. He never laments over losses.

He's a warrior. I think the reason I was able to believe I could do it again was due to the fact that I had him to go through it with. My husband gives me hope for all men. You really can fight the good fight, men. You really can offer your strength to a woman, and in return receive her whole heart.

This time around I became very specific in my prayers. You see, I was beginning to really own my identity as a daughter of God. He had come through before. I knew He would again. My prayer was this. Don't laugh at me, until the end, because you might want to try it out. I told God the truth. I said, "God, I really want another baby. But if you allow me to get pregnant again could it happen quickly and be an easy pregnancy, with no complications. Also, I would really like for this baby to be a boy."

We had recently moved and I was going to have to find a new OBGYN, so I added my request for a doctor to the list. "If you decide to give me this baby, I would really like to have a female OBGYN. I'd like her to be a Christian, and I want her to be the one who delivers the baby." I didn't want to have to take whoever was on call if I went in to labor when my doctor was off. I also added one more thing to the list. I even laughed when I said it. I said, "One more thing God, if you could please help me not gain a lot of weight this time. I want to look really cute with this pregnancy, and feel really good." I said, "I am open either way, if you choose to tell me that two kids are enough for me, that is fine. You are God and you know best. I just want to ask you ahead of time for these requests, just in case you want to know." I am happy to tell you that God gave me every single thing I asked for! I got pregnant quickly. I did not have one complication. I got my female, Christian OBGYN. I also gained the least amount of weight with this pregnancy. I felt the best I'd ever felt pregnant, and felt pretty cute if I do say so myself! I really believe God enjoys it when we include Him in everything. I know it might seem vain to ask God to let me feel cute with this pregnancy, but that is why I think God is so cool, He gets it. He cares about how we feel. With Kassidi, let's just say I celebrated a little too much being pregnant. I was a little 'puffy' with her. All that to say, I got my baby boy! Oh, did I mention my doctor was there to deliver him? Yes, all my requests were answered. I was overjoyed. My girls were over the moon excited to have their little baby brother. I guess it goes without saying, Kevin was thrilled to have a son! He was so cute with him. Kevin Charles Noonan the Second. We decided to call him Chaz, short for Charles. Oh my Chaz, he stole my heart right out of my chest! I was madly in love from the second I laid my eyes on that baby boy. I couldn't believe I had a boy. I came from a family of all girls. Me, the youngest of the three girls. Even my dog was a girl. My poor dad was totally out numbered. Now, just like I pictured Bathsheba doing, I'm looking down at this perfect tangible kiss from God of redemption to my soul yet again. Life was good. Real good!

It was so fun having three kids. I loved the craziness of it. I remember my mom saying, Valeri, "Everything is going to get harder. You will have way more laundry, need way more food, the house will be way more messy. If you have three kids, you might as well have five." I just laughed at her and said, "You had three kids and I don't remember ever seeing dirty laundry in the laundry room, or the house messy, and you always had three meals on the table every day." She laughed and said, "You have selective memory." I still don't think that was the case, I truly don't ever remember dirty laundry, or the house being messy. My mom was the most amazing mom when it came to all those things. She was right though, it was harder with three kids. As the months went on, I began to feel like it was becoming harder than I could bear. In fact, it was harder than I could bear. What I didn't realize then was, I was experiencing postpartum depression.

At first I just thought I was really emotional. Maybe my hormones were out of balance. Maybe it was because Chaz wasn't sleeping through the night every night. Then it started to get worse. I remember looking at Kevin one day as I sat on the sofa in the family room and I said something that made me even cringe once it came out of my mouth. I said, "I wish I could push hard enough into this couch that I would absorb into it and disappear. I can't do this Kevin, I don't deserve these beautiful kids, I don't deserve you. I can't be the mom I am supposed to be, or the wife I need to be. I *really* can't be a pastors wife, that's for sure." He looked back at me and said, "Val, what are you talking about? You are an amazing mom and an incredible wife. No one expects you to be the perfect pastor's wife." As nice as that was, it didn't help me. You see, I thought differently. I had some old narratives going on in my head.

When you experience depression – that dark cloud of depression- you don't have the luxury of hiding things anymore! It all bubbles up to the surface and there is no holding it back. What I didn't realize then was, this was the one gift I didn't ask for when praying about having another baby, but it was a gift I am glad God gave me.

How can I refer to depression as a gift? All I can say is that it saved my life. I am writing this book today because of that time that I went through. I am still married to my amazing husband and I have three incredible kids who blow my mind every day that I live and breathe. I don't deserve any of this. But I wouldn't have been able to completely enjoy these gifts from God if I hadn't accepted the gift of "Getting real."

It got so bad that I couldn't get out of bed. I would lay in that bed all day and night. I remember putting Chaz next to me in the laundry basket once he started sitting up, so he could play with his toys and I could lay in bed. Kevin would come home and, God love him, he'd clean up, feed the kids, and listen to me cry. The room stunk, I stunk, and I couldn't do anything about it. I remember it getting to a point where even I knew I needed serious help. I caught myself wondering how I could disappear. The lie that was going through my head over and over was, "You don't deserve these incredible kids, you don't deserve this amazing husband. They would all be so much better off if you were gone." I thought about how if I could drive my car on to the freeway, pull off to the shoulder, throw something out onto the freeway, get out, and run in front of the oncoming cars; it would look like an accident. This way, no one would have the trauma of thinking I killed myself. I could disappear, it would be the best thing I could do for my family. I knew that was not me. I never thought like that. I never had the desire to do something like that.

I finally told my OBGYN at my scheduled visit what

I had been going through over the last few months. I started to cry because I couldn't fake it anymore. After hearing my symptoms, she said, "Valeri, you're experiencing Postpartum depression. I can prescribe you a low dosage anti-depressant. You can take that for about six months and it should help level out your serotonin." She explained how this happens sometimes after pregnancy. I had been through a lot of pregnancies, and it can get worse with each pregnancy. I was appalled! Me, depressed? What? I was a Christian woman. Christian women don't need to go on anti-depressants. How dare her say that. She could tell I wasn't buying it. She then said, "Okay, well here's another option. You can go to the gym, get on a treadmill, turn it up to the highest level and run on that for an hour and see if that raises your serotonin levels enough. Or, you can just take this little pill once a day, and see how that works." Reluctantly, I agreed to take the stupid pill. At least, that is what I thought of the pill at the time. She didn't stop there. She also said, "I think you should consider going to a Christian counselor. You and Kevin are in ministry and it can be very lonely during times like this. It's hard to talk about these things when you're supposed to be the one helping everyone else." A Christian counselor? I was offended. Now she wants me to go to a shrink? What does she think I am, crazy?

I was devastated, but I didn't have a choice. I was in a bad state. So, I started taking the pills. They did begin to help. I also made an appointment with the counselor that my doctor recommended. Boy, was it nice to have that answer to prayer right about now. A Christian OBGYN during a time like this was a gift. As I began to see the Christian counselor, I started to realize I had some rewiring I needed to do. I remember when I sat in that counselors office one day, crying as usual. She looked at me and said something that changed my life forever! She said, "Valeri, do you know if all you can do is lay in your bed, stinky and unable to be the mother you think you should be, unable to be the wife to Kevin you think you should be, unable to be the pastor's wife you think you should be, but you let God love you, just the way you are, you are enough. He is pleased with you. He thinks you're enough." I thought she was crazy. I was so shocked by what she had just said, I stopped crying and just looked at her like, what?! All I could think was, "Oh, I get it, this is why people pay you the big bucks, so you'll tell them stuff like this. To make them feel better about themselves. To keep them coming back." As ugly as it was, I really thought that. And then she looked at me, and quietly, but very directly, said, "Valeri, that is all God wants from any of us. He just wants us to allow Him to love us. You love your children don't you?" Of course I loved my children. She knew that. But she pressed on, "Would you stop thinking your child was worthy enough if they couldn't do anything but lay in bed crying?" I shook my head, "No, of course I'd still love them."

I began a process called psychotherapy. I went to every one of the twelve sessions my therapist recommended. It was the most wonderful and most difficult thing I ever did. There were times I said to God, "How much more do you want from me? I feel like I'm stripped naked, with a spotlight shining on me, while a rototiller plows over me." You see, I was letting God set me free. I had made a vow to God earlier in my life, saying, "God, I want to do whatever it takes to be completely free from anything in my past - my families past, generational strongholds, or any curses that will keep me or my children from living life to the full." I was determined not to pass any of it on to my kids. They did not deserve to carry any of my baggage. Even baggage I didn't know about. I asked God to bring it to light so I could be free of it. Let me tell you, He did just that. It was the greatest gift I could have ever asked for.

I was set free during that time. But I had to choose freedom. There wasn't one day I could choose to camp on the side of victim or circumstance. I had to stay rooted and planted on the side of hope. I had to be a prisoner of hope. I'll never forget one evening when I was lying in bed, clicking through the channels on the television. I stopped when I heard a young preacher say something that seared down into my soul. He said, "Even if you can't stand up on the outside, stand up on the inside." The whole message poured like a pitcher of water called hope all over my dry, thirsty soul. I decided at that moment, to get up on the inside. I thought, "Valeri, you have to do something. You can't camp here, it isn't fair to your family, or yourself." On that day, I decided to get up. I thought, "I need to get out of this bed, I've got to do something different. If I'm going to be miserable laying in this bed, I might as well be miserable on a treadmill at the gym, getting healthy." Believe me, I would be miserable. I don't particularly love working out. I told Kevin I wanted to join the gym. He looked at me like, "Is your medicine out of balance?" It would've shocked him even if I had been perfectly healthy. We agreed that I would join the gym. Not only did I decide to go to the gym, but I decided I would get up and get my work out done before my kids went to school, that way I could be home to get them out the door.

Oh baby, I was miserable when I started! I was out the door before the sun was up and heading to the gym. Sometimes it felt like I wasn't going to be able to handle it. But I pressed on. Once I arrived at the gym, I would head straight up to the row of treadmills facing the back window. The entire back wall was all window looking out over the city. It was a perfect place for me to run because no one could see me. I would get on that treadmill and as I ran I would cry, asking God to please help me. Little did I know at the time, as I watched the darkness outside the window begin to illuminate from the rising sun, over the new day ahead, this image was also happening inside of me. As I ran on that treadmill, crying out to God, I was being set free. The Son was rising over my darkness. I was giving my mess over to the one who could turn it into something beautiful.

I began to get stronger not only physically, but emotionally and spiritually as well. I was starting to feel better. I continued going to my weekly counseling appointments. The rewiring was starting to work. As I began to do things differently in my thinking and behavior, the sun was slowly rising over my soul. I was becoming a new person, and it was a new day in my life. I was being set free. I didn't only recover from depression. I came out of it healthier and stronger than before.

You see, God used the depression to help me deal with the things I normally would have kept tucked away, under my blanket of pride. My trying to be the "Professional Christian" kept me hiding. He also used the process of medicine, counseling, and exercise to show me how to access the power, love, and self-discipline that is mine to access. 2 Timothy 1:7 says, "I have not given you a spirit of fear, [timidity, anxiousness, cowardice] but of power, love and self- discipline." I am so thankful God didn't give me an immediate miracle of healing. It was through the process of my healing that I found out what I needed to keep, and what I needed to let go of. I needed to let go of worrying about what others thought of me. I needed to allow the approval of God over my life to be the only approval I needed to feel I was enough. I needed to let go of thinking I had to be perfect or I wasn't valuable. I realized how much God cared about the smallest details of my life. I finally understood how much God cared about my heart. I realized I had to guard my heart from the lies of the enemy. I also realized how powerful it is to be completely real. To be fully known and not feel the need to hide any part of me. If someone couldn't handle all of me, they didn't deserve any of me. If God could handle everything about me and still love me unconditionally, that was all that mattered.

I also found out how powerful my choices are. I had to choose to listen to the doctor and take the medicine. I had to make the call and set an appointment with the counselor. I had to make the financial sacrifice to complete the recommended twelve sessions. I had to keep showing up even when it was hard, even when I didn't want to face it anymore. I had to keep getting up out of that bed I wanted to stay in and push myself to get to the gym. I had to keep crying out to God. I had to tune my ears to listen to what God was speaking to me. I had to surround myself with people, messages, books, and music that uplifted my soul and motivated me to keep going. And I had to keep a very diligent watch over what I allowed my mouth to speak. I began to speak life over myself. I began to declare aloud daily, that I was strong, healthy, happy, beautiful, loved, enough, going to new levels, energetic, successful. I declared that I was not depressed, and never would be again. I declared the stronghold of depression broken over me and my family. My children will never be depressed because it was stopped with me. Before I saw it happen, I declared it.

The gift of freewill that God gave us is so powerful. It is the most powerful force in the universe, next to God, of course. But that is what separates us from any other living creature. We were created in the image of God. You can change your whole life by choosing to think and behave differently. The reason things change is because of the way you choose to look at things. Nothing has to change around you right now in order for your life to change. You just need to reframe it.

Anyone that tells you being a Christian is the easy street isn't telling you the truth. Anyone that tells you being a Christian is boring isn't telling you the truth. And especially, anyone that tells you being a Christian isn't the most wonderful life a person can ever live, isn't telling you the truth. I feel like I have lived the best life anyone could ever live. Yes, even with the challenges. Heck, I haven't even shared all of them. But that is what makes it so sweet. I have things to talk about with Jesus when I get to heaven that only we know about. I get to thank Him for the times He met me and cared for my heart. I get to laugh with Him about the time when He gave me all the things I asked for. I get to say thank you! I can't wait to see Him. However, if I never went through anything with Him, I wouldn't really know Him.

Reframing life on this earth as our opportunity to get to know God will help you live each day with intention. Reframing things always changes things. You see, once in heaven, I can't believe for a miracle anymore. I won't need one anymore. I can't ask Jesus to show me a sign that He is with me, because I will see Him face to face. I won't have the opportunity to bring the sacrifice of praise to Him, when I really don't feel like praising Him, because I'll always want to praise Him. You see, our only chance to make memories with Jesus is now, on earth. This is our only chance to show Him what He did on the cross really was enough, by living like it now. Taking Him up on it when he says, "Come to me all you who are weary, and heavy laden, and I will give you rest, take my yoke upon you, because my yoke is easy, and my burden is light" (Matthew 11:28). Even when it hurts, once you resign your old narrative - your old yoke of slavery, and burden of shame - your life can be light and easy. Even when it hurts, you will have joy and you will be able to praise Him.

Allowing God to heal our hearts will take courage. It isn't always easy to heal. It is much like healing after a major surgery, it takes time and requires dealing with some discomfort in order to heal completely. However, most people I know will choose to have surgery regardless of the down side the healing process requires because they know in the end it is worth it. It is no different in the healing process of our heart. Our emotional, mental, and spiritual healing of the heart requires work, discomfort, and determination. It is so worth it.

CHAPTER NINE

Choose to Finish Strong

WE SEE WITH DAVID that he didn't recover from his mistakes. He never came back strong again. Bathsheba was the opposite. She became stronger through pain. She allowed God to fight for her. She did the things that were not comfortable - being gracious to David and continuing to walk with her head held high, doing the right thing when all the wrong things were happening to her. She put all her heart into raising her sons to love God with all their hearts. She was relentless with Solomon. Over and over again in the Proverbs, you see the warning of not allowing yourself to be led away and destroyed by lust. It seems this was a common theme Solomon must have heard repeated to him many times in order to write about it in such depth. Unfortunately, as we see so often, people can be instructed in the ways of God, they can read the

Bible and even pray; but if there is no application of the instruction, it won't help.

Solomon was given a lot of instruction. He was taught to love wisdom. To desire wisdom over wealth, wisdom over everything else. I think that is why when God told Solomon he could ask for anything, and it would be given to him, Solomon asked God for wisdom. It was such a beautiful request from a young man. Yet, I don't think he came up with that all by himself. His mother had been drilling the importance of wisdom into him from a very young age. She didn't want to see him repeat the painful choices his father made. There was a lot of devastation in Solomon's family, and a lot of it could have been avoided by the simple presence of a strong father who would have stepped up and spoke up when his children needed him to. David never fully got his voice back after the sin with Bathsheba. It is a lesson for us all to heed. We don't have to allow the mistakes of our past to dictate our future. We do have to get out of the prison of shame the enemy wants to keep us in. We are forgiven the minute we repent and ask for forgiveness, but we have to receive the forgiveness and walk in it.

You see, Jesus will unlock the prisons of shame, fear, and anger, and show us the way out. But it is our responsibility to get up and walk out with Him.

There are many people that go through their entire lives forgiven by God for their sins, and yet, they choose to stay in the prison of the past. They allow the enemy to play old tapes of their past mistakes and failures. We have a responsibility to renew our minds and intentionally focus on who we are in Jesus. David needed to stop lamenting over his past failures. He also needed to open his mouth and confess his sins to others around him. If we don't own our stuff, our stuff will own us.

I believe David had some more confessing to do after he repented of his sins to God. He needed to confess his sins and ask forgiveness from the many people he hurt by sinning with Bathsheba. It seems he made things right with Bathsheba. We will never know for sure. It does say he comforted her. I hope there was an apology. However, there were many others that David needed to confess his sins to and ask for their forgiveness.

Bathsheba's grandfather, Ahithophel, saw everything David did to his granddaughter. He knew what David did to Uriah. David needed to go to him and repent. He needed to ask Ahithophel to forgive him. He needed to go to Eliam, Bathsheba's father, and make it right. He needed to confess to Eliam how sorry he was for causing so much harm to his daughter and son-in-law. He needed to go to Joab, the man David asked to order Uriah's death. He needed to go before the people of Israel and repent for sinning against God, and the people he hurt so badly. He also needed to stop the patterns of sexual addiction. He needed to confess his sin in that area and stop the cycle. You see, the minute David confessed his sin to those people, regardless of how they responded, he would have been set free from the guilt and shame. He wouldn't have to hide anymore.

It might seem like a risky thing for a king to do. Yet, it was the key that would have stopped the generational cycle of adultery, lying, secrets, and murder from passing down to the next generation. You see, if David had confessed everything, the enemy wouldn't have been able to keep him in the prison of shame he stayed in till his death. Because David remained quiet, the sexual sin and addiction, as well as murder, lying, and devastation was passed down to next generation. Why do I say this? As a counselor, I've seen the power of confession. When a parent owns their sin, as ugly and awful as it might be to have to confess it to your kids, something supernatural happens. The minute the parent comes clean, even if it hurts really bad to hear it, the kids are set free from the generational curse passing down. They have a choice to fight it. Maybe the parent is confessing infidelity in the marriage. Or maybe a mother carried shame for years because she had an abortion before her children were even born. God isn't holding it against them, the enemy is.

You see, there's something about secrets the enemy loves. He can keep you locked up in that prison of shame with him, even if the door to freedom is wide open. He knows the fear of rejection and disapproval is a powerful weapon. It doesn't make sense, but we've all been there. Many of you reading this might still be in that prison. The door is wide open; you love Jesus and you know Jesus loves you. However, you're still in that prison because the enemy has convinced you that you will face rejection if anyone else knows about your past. Isn't it funny how we can accept God's forgiveness yet allow the approval of people to hold us hostage? Get up and get out of that prison. Set your kids free from carrying your baggage into their future.

At the end of David's life, Bathsheba is still respected and loved by him. In the first chapter of 1 Kings, we see Nathan show up again to intervene on Bathsheba's behalf. David's oldest son, Adonijah, has decided to declare himself the new king of Israel - even though David is still alive. Nathan goes to Bathsheba and tells her what is going on. He is concerned for her and Solomon because he knows if Adonijah becomes the king, Bathsheba and Solomon will be killed. He instructs her to go to David and remind him of his promise. David had made a promise to Bathsheba that her son Solomon would be the successor to his throne as King of Israel.

In 1 Kings 1:15, we see Bathsheba go to David. As she was speaking to David, Nathan planned to enter and tell David the same story. This would ensure that David recognized the seriousness of what was going on. It would also remind David to do what was right before God.

David is now very old and on his deathbed. Scripture tells us he is so sick that there is nothing he can do to keep warm. The head servants find it helpful to bring David a young beautiful virgin, Abishag, to care for David in his last days, to lie with him and keep him warm. Gross! Yes I said it, gross! There is no medical condition that requires a beautiful young virgin to bring warmth to a dying old man. I wish this wasn't included in the scripture. However, it does show us again that God does not keep secrets. He does not withhold information from us just because it might make David look bad. No, David made himself look bad. He also doesn't withhold the ugly information with concern it will make Him look bad or give us license to sin because we see that David sinned. No, God expects us to use the brain He gave us. He must believe we are capable of handling the information.

God is the perfect example of a great father. He allows us to own our own choices. He will forgive us our sins that we confess. Yet, we have to walk in repentance as well as in the forgiveness. This part of the story is a clear indicator that David never fully renounced the sexual sin of his past. There was still a part of David that tried to fill the void of intimacy with lust. Come on, you can't tell me they didn't have dogs in those days. I have two dogs and they are very good at cuddling with me in bed and keeping me very warm. Bring him a dog! A wonderful, loyal, cozy, warm dog! Bring him as many dogs as he needs. I also wonder how it felt for Bathsheba to enter David's bedroom and even on his deathbed find he has a young, beautiful virgin lying next to him. Where were all his wives and children? Why would a stranger be the last person next to him, comforting him before he dies?

I also can't help but wonder, how many times did she have to forgive him? How many times did Bathsheba have to hand that hurt and anger over to God in order to keep a pure heart before him? I guess there's another lesson for us to learn from Bathsheba. We have to forgive the people that hurt us as many times as needed in order to stay free from bitterness. She clothes *herself* in strength and dignity. She doesn't wait for someone else to do it for her.

Seeing Bathsheba, David asks, "Bathsheba, What

can I do for you?" David loved Bathsheba. He wanted to take care of her even in his brokenness, up to the very end of his life. She explains what is happening and tells him if he doesn't act on his promise, she and Solomon will be treated as criminals and eventually killed. As she finishes speaking to David, Nathan enters as planned and tells the king the same story. Bathsheba is ushered out when Nathan enters. As soon as Nathan is done speaking with the king, David calls for Bathsheba.

I love this! 1 Kings 1:28 says, "King David responded, 'Call Bathsheba to me.' So she came back in and stood before the king. And the king repeated his vow. 'As surely as the Lord lives, who has rescued me from every danger, your son Solomon will be the next king and will sit on my throne this very day, just as I vowed to you, before the Lord, the God of Israel.'" Yay David! You did it! You finally spoke up and did what was needed for your wife and for your son! We also see Bathsheba responding to her husband with great respect and honor. In the next verse, it says that Bathsheba bowed low with her face to the ground and, kneeling before the king, said, "May my lord King David live forever!"

Not only did David tell Bathsheba he would fulfill his promise to her, he made sure it would happen that very day. Scholars say he was in the final stages of death, he was so sick and unable to keep warm. His body was shutting down. However, the mighty King David was back for the last few hours of his life. He didn't have someone else ensure his promise would be fulfilled, he did it.

He started barking orders, and people starting jumping. It was all for his wife, Bathsheba, and as he said, *her* son Solomon. He called for Zadok the priest, Nathan the prophet, and Benaiah, his personal body guard. He told them to take Solomon and his officials to Gihon Spring, Solomon was to ride on his mule. Once at Gihon Spring, Zadok and Nathan were to anoint Solomon the King over Israel. David instructed them to blow the ram's horn and shout, "Long live King Solomon!" David continued, "Then you are to go up with him, and he is to come and sit on my throne and reign in my place. I have appointed him ruler over Israel and Judah."

When Adonijah and his guests heard the celebrating and realized what was going on, Adonijah ran for his life. All of his guests jumped up in panic from the banqueting table and scattered. Solomon was the new king of Israel! David made it right! The celebration was so joyous and noisy, the earth shook with the sound. Wow! That is what happens when leaders do the right thing before God and their family. There is joy and celebration.

Now, the time was near for David to die and he gave a charge to Solomon. "I am about to go the way of all the earth," he said. "So be strong, and act like a man, and observe what the Lord your God requires: Walk in his ways, and keep his decrees and commands, his laws and requirements, as written in the Law of Moses, so that you may prosper in all you do and wherever you go" (1Kings 2:2-3 NIV). Those were the last words we ever hear from David. After David finished fulfilling his promise to Bathsheba, he died. He finished strong! The old King David had come back, even if it was only for a short time. He took care of the one wife he adored. He was not going to let her lose another son because of him. He had a chance to protect her heart, protect her life, and this time he was going to deliver. Even if he had to use every bit of feeble strength he had left. He did it. He fulfilled his promise to Bathsheba. He finished strong. What a beautiful mess.

Solomon was now king of Israel. What was going on in the heart of Bathsheba at that moment? I'm sure she was so proud of her boy, her Lemuel! He was her boy, devoted to and dearly loved by God. He was her gift from God. I wonder if she felt she had done all she knew to prepare her boy for the incredible job ahead. What a beautiful mess.

Adonijah returns on the scene and is petitioning

Bathsheba to bring a request before King Solomon on his behalf. Adonijah is still scheming and trying to manipulate a way to take the throne of David away from Solomon. I want to point out, as we briefly look at this account, how much credibility Bathsheba has even with this crafty son of David. "As you know," he said, "The kingdom was mine. All looked to me as their king. But things changed, and the kingdom has gone to my brother, for it has come to him from the Lord. Now I have one request to make of you. Do not refuse me." "You may make it," she replied. So he continued, "Please ask King Solomon - he will not refuse you - to give me Abishag, the Shunammite as my wife." "Very well," Bathsheba replied, "I will speak to the king for you" (1 Kings 2:17 ESV).

Now we arrive at my favorite verse in the entire account of Bathsheba. I have read this verse over and over for eight years and it still brings tears to my eyes each time I read it. 1 Kings 2:19-20 reads, "So Bathsheba went to King Solomon to speak on Adonijah's behalf. The king rose from his throne to meet her, and he bowed down before her. When he sat down on his throne again, the king ordered that a throne be brought for his mother, and she sat at his right hand. 'I have one small request to make of you, she said. I hope you won't turn me down.' 'What is it, my mother?' He asked. 'You know I won't refuse you.'" She went on to deliver Adonijah's request, knowing Solomon would deal with him wisely. How foolish Adonijah must have been, to play games with the two wisest people in the history of Israel, and think he would win.

Adonijah was requesting Abishag, the young woman called upon to attend to David at the end of his life. Adonijah was unrelenting in trying to find an inroad to the throne, and to getting rid of Solomon and Bathsheba. Although Abishag was not a concubine or wife of David, she was considered property of the king. Marrying Abishag could give Adonijah a legitimate claim to his father's throne. Bathsheba wasn't dumb to this deceptive request, she was confident that her son was wise enough to handle it well. Unfortunately, Adonijah was killed for his deceptive plan to steal the throne from Solomon. Adonijah had been overtaken with pride, secrecy, and a lust for power.

Again we see Bathsheba clothed in dignity and quiet strength. She didn't try to convince Solomon to do the right thing. She wasn't afraid of Adonijah, or the outcome of his schemes. She wasn't striving, she was trusting. She had strength that could only come from a woman who knew her God would never fail her. She had gone from being completely desolate, to sitting at the right hand of the King of Israel. What a beautiful mess.

Here is a picture of a man who loved his mother. This is a woman whose children rise and call her blessed. Bathsheba was crowned Solomon's queen. She was the queen mother of Israel. This was the highest honor any woman could ever be given. Why was she chosen out of all the women of Israel? It was because she was the wisest woman he ever knew. She was the woman of great wisdom, honor, virtue, and noble character. The virtuous woman. What a beautiful mess.

Bathsheba and Nathan continued to speak into Solomon's life throughout his years as king. It was once they both died, and without their guidance, that Solomon began to drift away from the teachings of wisdom. He began to take on the all too familiar sins of his father. He did this by taking many wives, and he eventually went to a much greater level than his father. He ended up taking 700 wives and 300 concubines. What in the world happened?

It goes back to the power of generational strong-holds. Yes, David finished strong by keeping his promise to Bathsheba. Yet, there were many years in which Solomon saw actions taken by his father that were not characteristic of a man after God's heart.

He saw his father remain silent when he should have spoken up. His brothers Amnon, Absalom, and Adonijah all died because of the strongholds of pride, lust, and secrecy.

David was a wonderful man after God's heart. In the Psalms, we see him being used to prophetically tell the heart of God to others. Both poetically and literally, he describes the despair of Jesus enduring the cross. God used David as a mouthpiece - to share His feelings, His pain, and His sorrows over sin. I believe David was able to pen those Psalms so passionately because he related so deeply to the pain of sin and despair. David is an example of someone striving to please God, going after God with all his heart. He was the most powerful warrior against injustice and against the enemy of the people of Israel. Yet, there was a crack in the armor. There was a place I think the enemy always knew he had access to - the place of pain from rejection. It was the area of insecurity and needing to feel loved. We all have the potential for a crack in the armor of our heart. That is why the scripture found in Proverbs 4:23, penned by his own wise son says, "Above all else guard your heart for it is the wellspring of your life" (NASV). Other versions say it this way, "Above all else guard your heart, for everything you do flows from it"

(NIV). and "Above all else guard your heart, for it determines the course of your life" (NLT), or "Keep thy heart with diligence, for out of it are the issues of life" (KJV).

CHAPTER TEN

The Unveiling of the Virtuous Woman

I WANT TO TAKE you now back to the very beginning of this book, back when my husband and I were talking about the Mother's Day sermon. We did end up sharing about Bathsheba and Solomon. My husband read the poem my son wrote about me being the 'perfect mom' to the congregation. After my husband read the card he invited me up to join him in delivering the message for the day. He said "Join me in welcoming the 'perfect mom' to the stage to share with me in today's sermon." I couldn't wait to get up there and clear up the glaring misinterpretation of me as the 'perfect mom.' I couldn't wait to explain what we were really doing in building that up so big. The last thing I wanted any woman to feel that day was inadequate or less than because she wasn't all those things.

I got to the stage and began to break down the truth behind the darling card my little adoring son had made for me. I wanted them to hear it again through the eyes of an innocent little boy who loved his mom so much. Of course in his eyes, I was perfect. Of course he thought I was a superhero. He was only a little boy and at the time he was dependent on me for just about everything. Mothers have the power to bring life, and also the power to bring death. I could have destroyed my son's heart if I had disregarded him; if I had been abusive and uncaring. His heart was so vulnerable and so dependent upon my affection. He needed his mommy's care and affection. Did I hit the mark every time? No way. None of us ever will. Thankfully God covers our weakness with His strength.

Chaz's perception of me and my perception of me were quite different. But it made me think of God's truth. How does God see me? God sees all I do and adds His grace to it so it becomes beautiful. God sees my mess and creates beauty out of it. I never understood God's love for me, until becoming a parent.

We broke down the passage of Proverbs 31 and encouraged them to see it through the lens of a son writing about his beloved mother. We said, think of

Solomon writing this about his mom. A son, who chose his mother to be his queen. A son who when he became The King of Israel, would rise and bow down to his mother when she entered the room. Let's highlight Proverbs 31:10-31, "Sayings of King Lemuel," keeping in mind the card my son Chaz made for me.

Epilogue: The Wife of Noble Character

> A wife of noble character who can find?
> She is worth far more than rubies.
>
> Her husband has full confidence in her
> and lacks nothing of value.
>
> She brings him good, not harm,
> all the days of her life.

I believe this speaks to what Solomon would have seen in the relationship between David and Bathsheba. She could have done him harm, she always had the choice and option to. Instead she chose to forgive him and bring him good. As a result he had full confidence in her. Solomon saw how David adored her, and respected her. He also knew what he did to her.

VALERI NOONAN

She selects wool and flax
　　and works with eager hands.

She is like the merchant ships,
　　bringing her food from afar.

Isn't this like Chaz saying I make him a hot breakfast
with pancakes, eggs, and bacon *every* morning?

She gets up while it is still night;
　　she provides food for her family
　　and portions for her female servants.

She considers a field and buys it;
　　out of her earnings she plants a vineyard.

She sets about her work vigorously;
　　her arms are strong for her tasks.

She sees that her trading is profitable,
　　and her lamp does not go out at night.

This verse makes sense if we're seeing it from the
perspective of a little boy. A boy that goes to bed and
all he knows is that his mom is still up long after he
falls asleep. And when he awakens in the morning,
she's already up and getting breakfast ready.

A BEAUTIFUL MESS

In her hand she holds the distaff
    and grasps the spindle with her fingers.

She opens her arms to the poor
    and extends her hands to the needy.

When it snows, she has no fear for her
    household;
      for all of them are clothed in scarlet.

She makes coverings for her bed;
    she is clothed in fine linen and purple.

Her husband is respected at the city gate,
    where he takes his seat among the elders of
    the land.

She makes linen garments and sells them,
    and supplies the merchants with sashes.

This reminds me of the time when I surprised Chaz and redecorated his room. He loved the movie, "Cars" so I made that the theme. A quick trip to TJ Maxx can turn a mommy into a super hero. I found pictures, pillows, and décor items to go along with the theme. I even found a matching area rug. When Chaz walked in and saw his room he was blown away. He looked at me and said, "How did you do this mom?" He thought I had super powers. Chaz is a fifteen year old now and talks about it to this day.

> She is clothed with strength and dignity;
>   she can laugh at the days to come.

> She speaks with wisdom,
>   and faithful instruction is on her tongue.

> She watches over the affairs of her household
>   and does not eat the bread of idleness.

> Her children arise and call her blessed;
>   her husband also, and he praises her:

> "Many women do noble things,
>   but you surpass them all."

Solomon saw her way of dealing with people; her quiet dignity and kindness to others. He saw her ability to speak wisdom to them and her ability to laugh at the days to come because she does not let fear tell her what they will be like. Solomon calls her blessed. Even her husband adored her and praised her. She does not surpass all women because she is better than them. Rather, she surpasses them, in Solomon's mind, because she is Solomon's mom. She holds a special place in his heart as the one that loved and nurtured him. Again, looking from God's perspective, our relationship with Him is what washes us clean from unrighteousness. Our relationship with Him and belief in Him gives God a perspective of us as being pure and spotless, covered by grace.

> Charm is deceptive, and beauty is fleeting;
> but a woman who fears the Lord is to be
> praised.

> Honor her for all that her hands have done,
> and let her works bring her praise at the city
> gate.

Solomon wants others to see and praise her. She showed him that beauty is fleeting, that beauty cannot get you very far, that beauty is not something to chase while throwing aside all morals and convictions. Bathsheba is the example to the wisest man who ever lived of what a "noble" wife would look like. When I read the account of the virtuous woman from the perspective of an adoring son, all of a sudden, it becomes one of my favorite passages of scripture! Knowing Bathsheba is the virtuous woman makes this woman someone I can relate to because her life was very far from perfect. Much like Chaz in his acrostic penned about me, I liken some of these acclaims of the virtuous woman to the same heart of a boy that adores his mama and yet, doesn't see everything behind the scenes.

It turned out to be a wonderful Mother's Day message after all. The women were encouraged and amazed. God used the discovery my husband made about King Lemuel to ignite a hunger and passion in me and I began to research everything I could find out about Bathsheba. I hope you've enjoyed getting to know Bathsheba better. I have spent a lot of time wondering how Bathsheba lived so virtuously in the face of so much pain and suffering. Yet, after walking through some of my own times of difficulty, I think I've learned what it seems she knew all along. I have to choose every day to clothe myself in strength. I have to receive everything I need for each day as it comes. I can't rely on yesterday's supply of strength, energy, forgiveness or peace to get me through today. I have to choose to allow God to refresh me each and every day. Don't miss the vindication of God over your circumstance because the enemy is telling you it is too late or telling you God won't come. He's a liar! Jesus says it is never too late to begin again. God will never walk away, and He tells us to choose life every day. "Today I have given you the choice between life and death, blessings and curses. Now I call on heaven and earth to witness the choice you make. Oh, that you would choose life, so that you and your descendants might live" (Deuteronomy 30:19 NLT).

We really do have the power each and every day to walk in the blessed life. God wants it so badly for us, but He won't force anything on us. We have to be intentional about the life we live. I can't force my children to eat the healthy breakfast they need each morning, they have to choose to eat a nutritious meal. Similarly, God doesn't force His children to take the blessing He offers. But He does offer it to us, each and every day. Philippians 4:13 says, "I can do all things through Christ who strengthens me." He doesn't even ask us to do it in our own strength. He promises we can do it because He will give us His strength. What are you choosing today? Are you waking up in the morning and simply eating whatever the enemy serves up?

I had a picture come to my mind that really helped me when I was needing to make this a priority in my life. I felt God put the picture of a butler standing next to my bedside in the morning holding a platter filled with things for me to eat. Before my eyes were barely open he began to say, "Good morning, here is your breakfast, now eat it, eat it!" He is very forceful and I can barely see what's on the tray but I start to eat it because he is so persistent. Once I start eating what is on the tray, it occurs to me that what I'm eating is not good. The butler represents the enemy. He is right there in the morning, before you even get your eyes open. Before you are fully awake, he starts serving you up dread, fear, hopelessness, regret, shame, and insecurity about the day ahead. You name it, he serves it. He serves it up so fast you can barely recognize what is going on until you're filled up.

There was another butler standing next to him. He was very nice, calm, and not at all pushy. His platter looked so lovely. He smiles warmly and says, "Good morning, I have everything you need for today, are you ready to receive it?" He doesn't shove it in my face. He waits patiently until I am ready to receive it. He then serves me gently and gives me every-thing I desire. This is Jesus. He is there every day as well. Every morning, he stands and waits. He is holding everything you need to satisfy you and get you successfully through the day. Which platter will you choose? That was the question I felt like God was asking me. From that day on, I decided I was going to choose wisely. You see, we have the choice to have a great day every day. Not a struggle free, pain free day every day, but a great day every day.

I began praying a prayer that I now pray automat-ically before I am even fully awake. I begin receiving everything I need for the day before I get out of bed. I say, "Lord, I receive your love today, I receive your peace, your strength, your energy, your creativity, your approval over me, your favor, your power to open doors before me, and your protection to keep me safe." It might sound a little different from day to day depending on what I need that day. I push the death platter of the enemy right out of the way and welcome the platter of life. It works! We are graced by God every day, with everything we need to get through the day, strong. Yet, we can miss out if we don't choose to receive it.

What about you? Have you received the grace you need today? Have you been leaving the platter of grace untouched and walking through your day starving for the peace, energy, hope, confidence, provision, healing, and joy that was yours to take? I encourage you to take hold of everything that is rightfully yours. When your eyes open each morning before you do anything, receive what you need. Receive from Jesus whatever you need to get through your day strong.

I hope the beautiful mess of Bathsheba's life has given you hope. I hope it has shown you there's no circumstance that is too hard or too impossible to get through. Not only can you get through, but you can come out stronger and more powerful.

As we wrap up this journey of discovery together,

I find it appropriate that we end on the passage of scripture that inspired it all. If you're like me, you've tried to avoid this portion of scripture as much as possible until now. I'm hoping if that is the case, your feelings have changed. I hope now, you are as excited to go back to it as I am to take you there. I love this passage of scripture. It has become one of my favorites in the entire Bible. Proverbs 31 - the place we go to find the 'Virtuous Woman,' the 'Proverbs 31 Woman,' the 'Perfect Woman.' Fortunately, now we turn to that all too familiar passage with a new respect and appreciation for a woman who makes us all aware of how much God loves us. How God sees us, and how He cares so intimately about our heart.

Bathsheba, the woman who understands your pain. The woman who understands the sting of the betrayal you've experienced. The woman who mourns with your aching heart as you bury your precious child or your husband who you loved with every fiber of your soul. The woman who feels like every ounce of life has been sucked out of her desperate, breaking heart. The woman who understands what it feels like to be lied about and falsely accused. The woman who knows what it feels like to be taken advantage of and devastated, with no one to speak up for her. The woman who knows what it feels like to be sexually abused and left alone. The woman who knows what it feels like to lose the wonderful family who loved and cared for her so deeply. The woman who once had a life that was enviable. The woman who had a life so full of promise for the future, only to have it torn away from her all in one night. A woman who had to choose to believe God was still a good God even when everything around her was screaming the opposite.

This is the woman we can all look to and find the strength to clothe ourselves in dignity. She shows us how to hold our head up high and walk with grace. She shows us how to even laugh at the days ahead. The source of her strength was her God. The God who came to her rescue when no one else could, and no one else would. He came and He cared for her. He redeemed her. He elevated her to the highest place any woman could be held, and He made her the Queen of Israel. This woman shows you and me how God sees us. You may identify with the negative things Bathsheba went through. However, if this book teaches you anything, please let it be the truth of how God sees you. Right now as you are reading this book, He is smiling over you. He is crying with your broken heart. He is longing to step in and rescue your wounded soul. You are His precious daughter. He sees you as the queen He created you to be. He is offering you the title He has always had over your name. Queen _Aleen_ . Write your name there and start believing the truth. You are His queen. Bathsheba understands what it feels like to have a false identity placed over her true identity. The enemy wanted the word 'shame' to be written over her true identity of Virtue and Honor. However, God never allowed that to happen.

He gave her the title of, 'The Virtuous Woman.' That has never changed. The woman whom the wisest man who ever lived, King Lemuel, chose to be his queen. 1 Kings 2:19, "When Bathsheba went to King Solomon to speak on Adonijah's behalf. The king rose from his throne to meet her, and he bowed down before her. When he sat down on his throne again, the king ordered that a throne be brought for his mother, and she sat at his right hand."

Solomon's love for his mother is a picture of God's love for you and me. Solomon saw through the lies, the pain, the rejection, and the shame. He saw a beautiful woman. He describes this woman as so perfect, she is unattainable to any real woman. Yet, that is how God sees you and me. He sees you covered in the blood of Jesus that washes over every part of your life. He sees you perfect! That is why He will never allow the enemy to lie about you and put a title of shame over your heart, if you will just let Him in. Let Him take over. Stop pushing Him away and surrender your broken, tired, and hopeless heart over to His big, loving, and fiercely protective heart. Begin again, just as Bathsheba had to do. Bathsheba grew up in one of the most prestigious families in all of Israel only to have it all stripped away from her. She could have walked away from God at that point. Many would not have blamed her for it. However, she was a wise woman. I believe she decided to put everything God said to the test. God says He will never leave us. He says He will protect and vindicate His children. She opened her broken heart to God and allowed Him the chance to mend it. As we see from the story we just read about David and Bathsheba, God came through for her. God redeemed her mess and gave her beauty beyond measure. We end this story with the true identity of Bathsheba. Queen Bathsheba seated at the right hand of her son Solomon, the wisest man who ever lived. He honored her, and he loved her more than any woman.

At the end of Solomon's life, he comes to his senses and remembers the teachings of his mother and father. In Ecclesiastes 9:9, Solomon writes, "Live happily with the woman you love through all the meaningless days of life that God has given you under the sun. The wife God gives you is your reward for all your earthly toil." The man with 700 wives and 300 concubines returns to the teaching of his youth. It sounds very similar to the instructions he was given most likely by his wise mother in Proverbs 5:18-19, "May your fountain be blessed and may you rejoice in the wife of your youth ... may you ever be captivated by her love" (NIV).

The end of Ecclesiastes sees Solomon return to the last words his father ever spoke to him, "Fear God, and keep his commandments, for this is the whole duty of man." He then adds his own words to the conclusion. "For God will bring every deed into judgment, including every hidden thing, whether it is good or evil" (Ecclesiastes 12:13 KJV).

David was a man who went hard after the heart of God and he found it. He didn't have to be perfect, he just had to keep going back to the heart of God. David was the most valiant warrior for God. He single-handedly took down the most powerful giant in all the land. Not with a weapon of war, but with the unbending weapon of faith in his God. He truly believed God was the almighty, all powerful, one and only God. David was the person in the Bible who displayed throughout his life, such a passionate, authentic relationship with God. He included God in the highs of life and went straight to God with the lows. He was real with God, and God loved it. God never stopped loving David when he messed up. God never left David, even when David stepped away from

Him. That's what is so incredible about God. He never gives up on us. Ever. Even when we give up on Him. He still allowed David to be known as the man after His own heart. Why? Because as we have learned from this story of David, although David made some terrible choices, and experienced the consequences from those poor choices, he kept coming back to God. He humbled his heart and brought the glory back to God. The last thing David did on this earth before he died shows us the true heart of David. He rose up on his deathbed, and fulfilled his promise to Bathsheba. The last thing David did was protect Bathsheba and her son Solomon. He vowed to her he would fulfill the promise he made to her before God. And through fulfilling that vow to Bathsheba, David gave a charge to their son Solomon. He told Solomon to be strong and act like a man. He told him to observe what the Lord God requires in the Law of Moses so that he would prosper in all his ways. Jesus calls himself the offspring of David. "I, Jesus, have sent my angel to give you this testimony for the churches. I am the Root and the Offspring of David, and the bright Morning Star" (Revelation 22:16 NIV).

Solomon was a man who loved his mother with all his heart. He not only loved his mother, he honored her. He was determined to show the world her true identity. By choosing Bathsheba as his Queen, he was telling all of Israel and the world to come, this is a woman who is to be praised. She is a noble and virtuous woman. The wisest man who ever lived gave credit where credit was due. Her children rise and call her blessed (Proverbs 31).

Bathsheba faced a great deal of pain and devastation. She was given the opportunity to die as a very bitter, desolate woman. Instead, Bathsheba chose wisdom and trusted God with her whole heart. She didn't have a perfect life, and she faced unbelievable hardships. Yet, Bathsheba faced those hardships with strength and dignity. How did she manage to do that? She did not draw from within herself, she clothed herself with strength and dignity. Clothing is a covering for nakedness. She covered her naked and desolate heart with the dignity and strength of God. Therefore, she was a woman who could laugh at the days to come; she could laugh without fear of the future. Bathsheba did not strive, she waited quietly for God to deliver her. God never let her down. Bathsheba did not become a bitter and desolate woman. Instead, she became the most powerful woman in all of Israel. The King, her beloved Lemuel, called for a throne to be placed at his right side, next to him, because she was his queen. Queen Bathsheba.

As we come to the end of this journey of discovery together, I hope you have been encouraged. I hope you have found yourself in this story. I hope you've been able to find God in this story. Maybe you've discovered God for the first time. Or, perhaps like me, you've discovered a deeper appreciation of God. The God who is an intimate, loving father, always watching over our hearts. He cares about every detail and is fiercely protective over you and me. There is no pain too deep, no abuse too horrible, no loss too desolate, no betrayal too devastating, no sickness too powerful, no shame too condemning, no fear too debilitating, no lie too convincing, and no brokenness strong enough to break you. God is all powerful, all loving, all forgiving, all redeeming, all knowing, and madly, fiercely in love with you and me. I love how detailed God is. He doesn't miss a beat. Not one beat of your precious heart. He numbered them before He placed you in your mother's womb. He has a plan for you and me. Every beat of your heart plays a beautiful melody in the chambers of Heaven. Every beat counts. Let's not waste one more beat trying to manage this life on our own. You see, without God it's just a mess. However, with God it becomes beautiful, A Beautiful Mess.

It is with great honor I reintroduce you to Bathsheba. Please rise for the formal introduction of Queen Bathsheba, the Virtuous Woman of Proverbs 31.

CPSIA information can be obtained
at www.ICGtesting.com
Printed in the USA
FSHW010501280921
85069FS